Growth through Worship

GROWTH THROUGH WORSHIP

Alan Dunstan

BRITISH AND FOREIGN BIBLE SOCIETY
Stonehill Green, Westlea, Swindon, SN5 7DG, England

A catalogue record for this book is available from the British Library
ISBN 0564 08865X

Typeset by BFBS Production Services Department (TP Section)
Printed in Great Britain by Biddles Ltd, Guildford
Cover design by Litchfield Morris, Gloucester

Bible Societies exist to provide resources for Bible distribution and use. The
British and Foreign Bible Society (BFBS) is a member of the United Bible
Societies, an international partnership working in over 180 countries. Their
common aim is to reach all people with the Bible, or some part of it, in a
language they can understand and at a price they can afford. Parts of the Bible
have now been translated into over 2,000 languages. Bible Societies aim to
help every church at every point where it uses the Bible. You are invited to
share in this work by your prayers and gifts. The Bible Society in your
country will be very happy to provide details of its activity.

CONTENTS

To all those who

worshipped with me

in the Diocese of Gloucester

1978–93

1 THE MEANING OF GROWTH

Estate agents in rural areas often have among their advertisements small chapels somewhat ironically described as *converted* to domestic use. "Redundant" is a word that has been applied to churches – as well as to people – up and down the land. You do not have to go far in order to see a building once used for worship now standing derelict or put to secular use. The message to the public is of a church in decline.

Of course there were too many buildings. Some are no longer needed because the divisions which caused them to be built have happily been healed. Others are no longer needed because there has been a shift in population, or because in a mobile society, most people can travel a bit further in order to attend worship. And, of course, the church is more than buildings. It is not dependent upon special buildings. At a dedication festival or church anniversary we may sing:

> *Jesus, where'er thy people meet*
> *There they behold thy mercy-seat*

without realizing that the hymn was composed not for a church, but for something more like a meeting-room or hall. The church can meet in halls or houses; sometimes it does so now by necessity, sometimes by conviction. The buildings which have been made redundant or put to other uses were not all full at the same time. But when all that has been said, churches as a whole are emptier than they were a century ago.

Statistics speak mostly of decline. People look around the congregations to which they belong and wonder whether there will be enough members in 30 years' time (or less) to continue its life, and to meet the formidable demands made for the upkeep of the building. The principal characteristic of a Christian congregation is that it meets for *worship* and from this all its other activities are derived. The obvious need of most congregations is *growth* if they are to continue to be worshipping communities. The principal characteristic and the obvious need are brought together in this book which asks how there can be growth *through* worship.

GROWTH OF PEOPLE

"I suppose you have come to find out why we don't come to church,
Vicar" was a remark once often addressed to clergy when "visiting".
It is not now likely to be heard; nor are such visits often likely to be
made. Maybe there are still places where house-going parsons make
church-going people; but most clergy find that the visits they must
make for specific reasons absorb most of the time that can be allotted
to such exercises. Congregations may still hope for a minister who
will increase the size of the worshipping community, but most no
longer regard this as solely the minister's function. They see
themselves as involved in the process.

During the twentieth century, many efforts have been made to
reverse the decline in church-going by changes in worship. Great
claims were made in the 1930s for the hymn-book *Songs of Praise*.
Some believed that its theological stance and the freshness of its
language would appeal to progressive and thoughtful people. After
the Second World War, the wastage in confirmation candidates
and young adults exercised the churches; so in the 1950s, we
had Geoffrey Beaumont and the Twentieth-Century Light Musical
Group. *The Enemy is Boredom* was the title of a book by
Guy Daniel; it showed an empty church on its front cover and a full
one on the back, and the pages in between told the success story.
This was not the only book to record increased congregations
through a revolution in worship.

Such stories may still be told. "Family services" in many churches
attract sometimes dramatically larger congregations than those found
in more conventional forms of worship. The enemy is still boredom,
and we still seek to retain the interest and enthusiasm of those who
drift away from worship in their late teens. But all this concerns only
a small percentage of the population. We cannot speak to the
majority of people about "coming back to church" because they were
never there anyway. In *The Use of Hymns,*[1] I made some suggestions
about the choice of hymns for weddings, but have since heard from
many ministers that unless the couple are worshippers, they know no
hymns from which to make a choice. The same is true of services for
scouts or cadets. They may just remember "Lord of the dance" or
"Morning has broken" but not much else. They did not learn hymns
at school, and they were not in church to hear them. In speaking of
hymns, I speak of what has been the most popular of congregational
activities; if this is foreign territory, what of psalms, or prayers, or
sacraments?

There is no single or simple way by which we can fill churches with those hitherto unaccustomed to attending them. There are fundamental questions to be tackled – the possibility of God, the broad truth of the Christian message, and a sense of its relevance to life in today's world. And when people begin to show some interest in these things, there remains the matter of commitment. Whatever commentators may say of the original meaning and present application of the Parable of the Sower, it still seems descriptive of those whom Christ calls to be his disciples.

But it would be foolish to suppose that the style of worship in our churches has no bearing upon the size of the congregations. An imaginative act of worship will speak to people in a way that the reverse does not. That which is shoddy, dull, and careless is bound to repel; we have all been to churches which left us wondering how long we could worship if there were no alternative. Moreover, there are still occasions when people who are unfamiliar with Christian liturgy encounter some part of it. One chapter in this book will examine "rites of passage" such as weddings and funerals; it will ask whether they could be more luminous of that part of the gospel which they seek to reflect, and whether there are other occasions in human life that could be marked liturgically. Another chapter will be concerned with those acts of worship which still attract people who are at best very irregular churchgoers: carol services, Remembrance Sunday, and even "Songs of Praise".

It is important for any Christian community to recognize the limitations of its own concepts and styles. We must not suppose ourselves to be fully informed about all matters of worship, and expect newcomers automatically to conform to what we do. Perhaps there are still congregations which receive new members on their own terms, and expect them to appreciate what they find without asking awkward questions. But there are also, in many congregations, some who are by no means wholly satisfied with the worship they regularly experience, and are ready for change. And there are even more who were suspicious of and even hostile to changes when they came, yet have come to realize that they have grown in some way, and that such changes were for the good of the community as a whole. When the *Alternative Service Book* (ASB) was introduced by the Church of England in 1980, there were those who asked, "But will it bring more people to church?" Perhaps it did in some places, and in others drove people away. But that was never the point of the change. It was concerned more with those already worshipping, and with the generation to come. What was true of the

Church of England was doubtless parallelled in other churches which experienced changes in their liturgical practice. Such changes did not always result in a growth of people, but sometimes in a growth in people. To this we now turn.

GROWTH IN PEOPLE

The revolution in worship that has taken place in the last decades of the twentieth century can facilitate growth in at least four ways. The first lies in its emphasis on comprehensibility. The abandonment of archaic language, both in the Scriptures and in most forms of worship, means the removal of one hurdle in comprehensibility. This is experienced in its most dramatic form in the Roman Catholic Church by the use of services in the vernacular rather than in Latin. At least we know what the Bible actually is saying. Of course the point can be exaggerated. When the New English Version of the New Testament was first published, scholars of the day pointed out that although the language might be that of our own century, the thought forms were those of the centuries in which the books were written. And there is no language that can present the Bible in such a way that it is immediately comprehensible, and requires no effort in understanding. The things of God will always be mysterious to us. But mystery does not mean mystification.

Secondly, contemporary styles of worship provide for much more involvement by the worshippers. It is not merely that people have a more vocal or physical part (reading lessons, taking intercessions, and so on) or that services often have more responsive material. The general design of worship makes the congregation much more than an audience or gallery of spectators; instead, they become a worshipping community – involved both in obvious and more subtle ways in what is going on.

Thirdly, there are signs of more realism in worship. *The Book of Common Prayer* (BCP) order of Holy Communion has an intercession that represents a world far removed from our own; it is, in fact, a fairly accurate reflection of Tudor society and Tudor presuppositions. We are becoming more human in our worship. The Baptist *Patterns and Prayers for Christian Worship*[2] includes under prayers for family life:

> *Where grief has come for a loved one, or where love is no more; where jobs or home are lost or health has failed; where neighbours or relatives make trouble and children*

> *are wayward; where one or other is left coping with more*
> *than they bargained for, and nobody laughs or sings.*

And the United Reformed Church (URC) *Rejoice and Sing* has at least one hymn referring to broken relationships – which affect every congregation and most families. Some 30 years ago, Michel Quoist taught us to be more human in our personal prayers, and this is now spreading into corporate worship.

Fourthly, our forms of worship are more ready to concede that there are questions to which there is no immediate answer, problems to which there is no instant solution, mysteries which cannot now be explained. We find evidence of this in some of our modern hymn-writers, and in the new songs of the Iona Community. There are questions in life which are unanswered and unanswerable. The Christian religion is not some neat piece of kit in which we can find instant remedies or the correct answer to every doctrinal and ethical dilemma.

Worship is a means by which we grow. It is not a form of escapism, an anodyne, or a kind of spiritual self-indulgence. There may be times when we need all three, but if we find them in worship, we must not suppose that this is what it is about. John Betjeman perhaps wrote some autobiography in his poem "Before the Anaesthetic":

> *St Giles's bells are asking now*
> *"And hast thou known the Lord, hast thou?"*
> *St Giles's bells, they richly ring*
> *"And was that Lord our Christ the King?"*
> *St Giles's bells they hear me call*
> *I never knew the Lord at all*
> *Oh not in me your Saviour dwells*
> *You ancient, rich St Giles's bells.*
>
> *Illuminated missals – spires –*
> *Wide screens and decorated quires*
> *All these I loved, and on my knees*
> *I thanked myself for knowing these*
> *And watched the morning sunlight pass*
> *Through richly stained Victorian glass*
> *And in the colour-shafted air*
> *I, kneeling, thought the Lord was there,*
> *Now lying in the gathering mist*
> *I know that Lord did not exist;*
> *Now, lest this "I" should cease to be,*
> *Come, real Lord, come quick to me.[3]*

Nothing that encourages us to hide from God or texts that make it easy for us to evade his claims upon us can be real worship – for us. Many Christians know that it is possible to go to church, yet never really to worship. For worship is an encounter with the *living* God.

But we must not make the mistake of supposing that we are always wiser than the generations before us. We must not allow ourselves to think they had no understanding of the Authorized Version, or that realism was missing from their worship. When people said "there is no health in us", many knew perfectly well what it meant. When they heard St Paul say "Now I see through a glass darkly", it corresponded with much of their experience. Moreover there are, almost certainly, elements of earlier worship which we have forgotten or discarded to our peril. The need for awe, reverence, and mystery have been noted by many people and sometimes found to be wanting in modern liturgies. Perhaps one of our besetting dangers is shallowness in worship with a corresponding casualness in the worshipper. We need to recall the opening sentence of the preface to the first *English Prayer Book* in 1549 which begins:

> *There was never anything by the wit of man so well devised, or so sure established, which in continuance of time hath not been corrupted: As, among other things, it may plainly appear by the Common Prayers in the Church, commonly called Divine Service.*[4]

What was true of past liturgies may also be true of those presently in use.

Again, growth does not mean that we evaluate every act of worship by what "we get out of it". Evelyn Underhill has some wise words about prayer:

> *Do not entertain the notion that you ought to advance in prayer. If you do, you will only find that you have put on the brake instead of the accelerator. All real progress in spiritual things comes gently, imperceptibly, and is the work of God... Remember the only growth which matters happens without our knowledge, and trying to stretch ourselves is both dangerous and silly. Think of the Infinite Goodness, never of your own state.*[5]

And all this can be applied to our participation in the worship of the Church. It is good to be thankful for new insights, for fresh experiences, for any renewal in understanding, or devotion, or love that worship brings. But if there have been no obvious benefits to us, it does not mean that the occasion has been without value. In counselling sessions it is not just the times that we feel better that constitute healing.

Further chapters in this book will be concerned with specific areas in which worship means growth in people – through the Word of God, the Sacraments, the way in which people make their own contribution, and the praise that they offer. But, always, worship must involve such growth because it is an encounter with the living God whose will for us is that we should advance to that maturity which is our destiny in Christ.

GROWTH THROUGH PEOPLE

If people grow through their participation in worship, then it is likely that they will better be able to communicate to others the real meaning of worship. We have already noted that more people are actively involved in the conduct of worship than was once the case. It is also true that more people are involved in the planning of worship, and that it is no longer the prerogative of a mysterious "they" (i.e. the minister and perhaps the organist). There are congregations in which "family worship" is both lay-planned and lay-led. This will increasingly happen in Anglican rural parishes if they are in large groups and it is thought desirable to have a service in each church about the same time. This has long happened in Methodist and other churches. But there are signs in Methodist congregations that the whole of worship may no longer be at the discretion of the preacher, but that often he or she will be asked to fit in with local arrangements. And, in many congregations, urban and rural, there is a worship committee studying local needs, and attempting to digest and process the plethora of material that is now offered for worship.

The result of all this is that a greater number of people understand what is required in worship, and are able to pass on knowledge and insights. They may need to do this for their fellow worshippers, and they will certainly need to do so for those less familiar with the customs of churches. It is arguable whether Sunday worship is the best way of introducing enquirers to the

Christian faith. What is not arguable is that there must be tactful and informed members of the congregation to help such enquirers when they are present. And it has been proved, time and again, that people are attracted to churches not just by the quality of the worship they find, but by the quality of the welcome and acceptance they receive.

In any case, worship cannot be an end in itself. Our chief end may indeed be to glorify God and enjoy him for ever, but the God whom we are to glorify and enjoy is the God who "so loved the world that He gave...". There is thus inescapable connection between worship and mission. If that connection had been more fully understood, there would have been no need for a decade of evangelism, and if it is recognized now, there need be no fearfulness or argument about the remainder of the 1990s. It is God's purpose that his love and liberating power shall be known on earth, and one special way in which it is made known is through human beings that he has created. If we regard worship as a duty or an activity in which we engage for our own benefit, we have scarcely begun to understand the meaning of the word. This chapter has already asserted that worship is contact with the living God; it is no less contact with the loving God, and we all become in some way witnesses to that love. The ways in which we make our witness are manifold, and it is absurd to suggest that everyone should do the same thing. During a political election campaign, not all party members go canvassing, but it is essential that some should do so.

We all have to understand that we are witnesses, and that the ways in which we witness will be varied. But such witness does not mean that we have solved all the problems about God, the world, and our own human life. In recent years, words like "pilgrim" and "pilgrimage" have been used, and in evangelism, we are inviting others to join in that pilgrimage. For us it means that we are on the road, but it also means that we have a long way to go. Many of us, like John Bunyan's pilgrim, do not yet see yonder wicket-gate, but we think we have seen yonder shining light.

Growth through people will mean growth of people – perhaps by ones and twos rather than by some dramatic influx of worshippers. Such growth involves trouble and patience. But that is akin to the way that God has treated us.

Questions

1. What do you look for in worship? Is it what you ought to look for?

2. What were the most "real" moments for you in last Sunday's service?

3. How do you help strangers to the church to enter into what is happening?

Notes

1. Alan Dunstan, *The Use of Hymns* (Kevin Mayhew, 1990).

2. *Patterns and Prayers for Christian Worship* (Oxford University Press, 1991).

3. John Betjeman, *Collected Poems* (John Murray, 1958).

4. Quoted in successive editions of the *Book of Common Prayer* under the title "Concerning the Service of the Church".

5. Quoted in Carol E. Simcox, *A Treasury of Quotations on Christian Themes* (SPCK, 1975).

2 THE WORD OF GOD

The cemetery was full. Burials took place only when a grave was reopened. The chapel was therefore very seldom in use, and its interior was both dusty and dreary. The officiating clergyman had not brought his service book with him, assuming the usual provision of cards or leaflets. But there were none. The only printed matter in the chapel was a dilapidated Bible on the reading desk, so the lesson was the only part of the service that he did not have to recite from memory.

In most places of Christian worship, the Bible is the one book that you may expect to find. Whatever customary adjuncts of worship may or may not be there, you should be able to find a Bible. In many churches, a large copy stands on a lectern specially designed for it; in some churches, a copy is provided for each worshipper; in others, the Bible is ceremonially brought in at the beginning of worship. There must be few places of Christian worship in which some part of it is not read on Sundays. And, besides the formal reading of lessons, sentences from it will often be used to introduce worship, quotations from it will occur in prayers and sermon, and paraphrases or reflections of it will be found in hymns and songs.

LESSONS AND LECTIONARIES

Many chapters of this book will be concerned in some way with the use of the Bible in worship. For some part of this one, we will concentrate on what used to be called *lessons*, but what are now more commonly described as *readings*.

Most Christian traditions now assume some kind of ordered and systematic reading of the Scriptures in worship. The Anglican discipline of daily morning and evening prayer was built around the reading of Scripture and the first English Prayer Book provided for the reading of most of the Old Testament each year, and most of the New Testament three times in the year. The ideal of 1549 was subsequently modified, but the principle has been maintained. There has been much writing about the "daily office" in recent years, new attempts to research its origins, and suggestions that the office of the future should not have such heavy Biblical orientation.[1] But the requirement of these daily services was primarily to ensure the comprehensive and systematic reading of the Scriptures.

The majority of people attended these services only on Sundays and special occasions. A Sunday sequence of Old Testament lessons was provided in 1559, but not until 1922 were there special New Testament readings. The people "slotted in" to whatever part of the New Testament was being read – except, of course, at times like Easter and Christmas. On Sundays they also heard the rather random readings called the "epistle" and the "gospel" in the first part of the Communion services.

In the churches which came to be "dissenting" there was no comparable provision. But the regard for Scripture was certainly no less. What was sought in 1549 had in some measure been achieved in the next century – namely the belief that people should read and study the Bible. Worship in the home was emphasized, and it would include at least a "chapter". So far as Sunday worship was concerned, the emphasis was on freedom; but central to the services was the reading and expounding of the Bible. "Lecturing", or verse by verse exposition of the Scriptures, was sometimes included in services as well as the sermon itself, but all depended upon the belief that the Bible should be read at home. The same belief was generally held among the Quakers where a reading from the Bible might not necessarily occur at the Sunday meeting.

Our own twentieth century has seen an increased use of lectionaries throughout the Christian Church. In recent decades, this has been largely due to the work of the Joint Liturgical Group, formed in 1963. Its membership was drawn from all the mainstream churches in Great Britain, and the Roman Catholics were at that time observers. The two-year sequence of Sunday readings which they produced four years later became, with variations, the eucharistic lectionary of the *Alternative Service Book*, and was similarly adopted by many of the churches repre-sented on the Joint Liturgical Group. The Roman Catholic Church showed no less enthusiasm for a new sequence of readings at Sunday Mass, and produced its own three-year cycle.

Lectionaries are never perfect. The use of the present ASB lectionary for more than ten years had revealed many weaknesses. There is some duplication; there is an undue emphasis on St John in Year One, and an absence of much narrative material from both Testaments. Attention to the last was drawn in the report *Patterns for Worship*[2] which underlined the importance of story

"not only in inner urban areas and with children". This has gone
alongside the development of "narrative theology" at a more
academic level. And at the same time, there has been a progressive
withdrawal from the strongly thematic approach to Sunday
readings held in 1967.

Of those who use the lectionary which we have discussed,
Anglicans seem to have been the most critical. Perhaps the main
reason for this is that in the other churches which have adopted it,
it is seen more as a guide than a master. It is not obligatory for a
Methodist or Presbyterian to stick to the lectionary, whereas
Anglicans go through some searchings of heart before changing a
lesson. The Joint Liturgical Group in 1990 produced a four-year
lectionary and the coverage of Scripture is very considerably
wider; "controlling" lessons (favoured in 1967) have disappeared;
though there are links between the three lessons provided on
Sundays, no one theme is dominant. With a few exceptions, each
year concentrates on one gospel.

The four-year lectionary was adopted by the Methodist
Conference in 1992, and is printed in the Baptist *Patterns and
Prayers for Christian Worship* (1991). But the new *Book of
Common Order* of the Church of Scotland prints instead the
Common Lectionary – a three-year sequence which encourages
more consecutive reading. This is close to the Roman Catholic
lectionary and that of the Episcopal Church of the USA. There are
signs that Anglican liturgical opinion inclines to this option,[3] but
questions have been raised about more local schemes of reading in
those seasons which lie outside the festival periods.

It is not within the scope of this book to weigh up the merits and
drawbacks of diffierent lectionaries, and certainly not to pronounce
judgement upon them. The fact that for some years, many of the
mainstream churches in the UK have followed a roughly similar
Sunday lectionary has had a unifying effect. This has been evident in
broadcast services; it has facilitated "exchanges of pulpit"; it has
meant that the various commentaries on the Sunday lessons have
been usable by more than one branch of the Church. At the same
time, the absence of the Roman Catholic Church from this scheme
has been serious. Maybe, we have to move in two directions at one
and the same time; we should look beyond these islands as
supporters of the Common Lectionary urge us to do; and we should
be prepared for more local variation than Anglicans have hitherto
found acceptable. But we must not forget that we also live in a
mobile society.

Before leaving this subject, there are three general considerations that need to be borne in mind. First, we do need to provide for a wide and systematic coverage of Scripture, and this means that a lectionary must be devised for a longer period than two years. Acceptance of some kind of common lectionary would be of great advantage to ecumenism and to a mobile society. Secondly, the lectionary must not be a strait-jacket which prevents all creativity and spontaneity; if someone wants to preach on Naaman, it should not be necessary to wait for three years for him to come up in the lectionary. Thirdly, no lectionary can of itself provide all the biblical material that is desirable for God's people. Lectionaries can never be fully comprehensive, and they must always assume the presence of the same people in the same place each week. What is read on Sundays in church must be supplemented by what is read at other times – by individuals, by Bible study groups, and other gatherings which value and use the Scriptures. This must be urged in days when, even among Christian people, there is widespread ignorance both of what is in the Bible and what it means. And attention must often be drawn to the proliferation of translations, and of notes, commentaries, and other aids to reading – often attractive and relatively inexpensive.

PRESENTING SCRIPTURE

The manner in which the Bible is presented in worship is as important as that which is chosen from it. The first thing to be said here is the most obvious and also that which is most frequently neglected. The reading should be of the best possible quality. No one should normally be called upon without warning to read a lesson, and reading should certainly not be regarded as the prerogative of those who hold certain offices in church or community. In its excellent section on "Reading the Bible", the introduction to *Patterns for Worship* affirms:

> *Reading needs training. Even in Family Services, it is wrong to have children reading who cannot be heard, or who read without understanding. The same should be true for adults.*[4]

Without such principles, there will be a devaluing of the practice of listening to Scripture being read, or of reading it well. And this, in turn, leads to a devaluing of Scripture itself.

But "lessons" read by one voice are not the only way in which Scripture can be presented. There are passages (e.g. Isaiah 63.1–9) which would lend themselves well to two readers. The Song of Songs is not likely to be chosen very often for a Sunday reading, but the *Revised English Bible* indicates how it might be read. The dramatic reading of the Passion story is now familiar to many congregations; not only does it involve their voices, but people often feel involved in the events in ways they have not before experienced. Such a story – and others – can be broken up by the use of chorales, songs, or hymns which can provide a commentary upon what is read. If the building so permits, it can be effective to read passages from different positions within it. And the stories of the Bible can be presented in mime or dance.

The involvement of the congregation can be achieved in many ways; most important of all is that they themselves are listening, attentive, and expectant. Most congregations think it appropriate to remain poker-faced throughout the reading of Scripture, but there is much humour in the Bible, so why not laugh when something funny is heard? I recall guffaws of merriment when Matthew 22.23–27 was read in a theological college. Did Jesus take it seriously when such a preposterous situation was put before him? This chapter is not recommending that congregations should take on the character of a pantomime audience, but surely Scripture because of its very variety requires variety in response. Of course there is the danger of over-dramatization, and of prima donnas making the most of their moment. But this danger seems to arise less often than that of dullness and insipidity. What matters above all is that the Bible is heard.

Two further points deserve discussion. One concerns the use of introductions to the readings. To the question of whether they should be used, the answer is probably "sometimes". When part of a long narrative from the Old Testament or the Acts of the Apostles is chosen, a brief indication of "the story so far" can be useful. Such introductions should be prepared with care, and in consultation with the preacher, so that they do not pre-empt the sermon or weaken its thrust. There is a strong case for an introduction to a difficult passage which is not going to receive much attention in the sermon.

Secondly, there is the question of whether or not people should be encouraged to "follow" the readings. In some churches, as we have noticed, there is a Bible in every seat, and the page on which the reading is found is announced. Some people find this a help in concentration, and it is obviously of great value to people who are hard of hearing. But it can be argued that, for the rest of us, there is real benefit in giving our full attention to listening, and allowing ourselves the full impact of read Scripture. Pew Bibles do remove any choice of translation, and if the Church of England is to have a lectionary that lasts longer than two years and is more flexible in character, it is unlikely that the successor to the ASB will have the Sunday readings printed in full.

PREACHING THE WORD

For Anglicans who use the ASB, it is now conventional for the reader to conclude with "This is the Word of the Lord" and the congregation to reply "Thanks be to God". The formula has been the subject of much criticism, and its invariable suitability has been often questioned. This conclusion to readings is not mandatory, and it is therefore curious that it is so generally used. But it does specifically involve the congregation in the reading and hearing of the Bible.

In the Church of Scotland and the English Free Churches, the formula has often been "The Lord bless to us this reading of his holy Word, and to Him be the glory" or some variant of that sentence – with or without a congregational "Amen". But it has been suggested that in the Reformed tradition, the reading and preaching of the Word go together, and the first is incomplete without the second. It would not be easy to devise a versicle and response that would be appropriate after *every* sermon, but the position of the Creed in some liturgies is significant in this respect.

It is certainly true that in contemporary liturgy, the sermon is closely related to the readings, and often follows directly after them. The arrangement has not been without its critics, but seems generally accepted. The advantages are obvious when the text or subject of the sermon comes from the last of the readings; rather less so when it is taken from an earlier reading or a sentence of Scripture used elsewhere in the service, and least of all if the sermon is "topical" rather than "biblical".

But few would disagree with the contention that the sermon bears some relationship to Holy Scripture. There is a broad theological (and sometimes pastoral) division between those who believe that preaching starts with the biblical revelation and seeks to apply it to the human situation, and those who prefer to start with some question related to the human condition, and ask what light the Bible sheds upon it. The majority of preachers may well vary their approach, but most would be happy with the brief explanation in *Patterns and Prayers for Christian Worship* which says that the sermon "brings together the Word, the worshippers and the world".

Perhaps the most remarkable thing about the sermon is its power of survival. Many years ago, Donald Coggan, who has done so much to encourage good preaching in the Church of England, wrote a book called *Stewards of Grace.*[5] In it he spoke of "Tom" who thought scientifically rather than biblically, who was becoming aware of other faiths, who was suspicious of the authority claimed for the Bible. The "Toms" of the world have multiplied since 1958, and not many are found in pews. But the reasons why he found it hard to listen to sermons have also multiplied. We are told that people are more accustomed to look than to listen; that the attention span of congregations is much less than preachers recognize; that dialogue is preferable to monologue, and discussion to authoritative pronouncement. Many alternatives to preaching have been proposed.

It must not only be admitted, but stressed that the pulpit is not the best place in which to deal with many subjects of Christian concern. It is not the best place in which to provide information; if the subject is the critical need of some stricken part of this world or the introduction of a new liturgy, it will demand questions. Nor is the pulpit the best place in which to discuss matters on which Christians hold different views – such as the possession of nuclear weapons or the morality of homosexual relationships. In no part of the Church does ordination give men or women the right to "hold forth" on any subject. In all parts of the Church, ordination does give them authority to preach the Word of God.

I recall two "sermons", both connected with the archiepiscopate of Robert Runcie. The first was delivered on the Sunday after his appointment was announced by a retired clergyman, who thought it was "a good thing". It seemed to me then, and it seems to me now, that the whole matter belonged to the intercessions rather than to the sermon. The second was of a very different order. It was preached at the time of Dr Runcie's retirement by one who had worked with him, and it was a thoughtful and moving tribute to the archbishop. I should love to have heard it on another occasion; but it did not seem to me an appropriate subject for a Sunday morning sermon, though parts of it might have been used to illustrate a sermon.

Sermons are laughed at, yawned through, and thought quite dispensable by many. But they survive. One reason for their survival is that the various bright alternatives to preaching are in the end occasional, and a succession of them cannot be guaranteed for every Sunday. But there is a better reason for their survival which is understood by some preachers, and appreciated by some congregations. This is when the sermon is regarded truly as a "breaking of the Word", which corresponds to the breaking of the bread in the Eucharist. The breaking of the Word means that all are being nourished in some way by the Scriptures, recognizing their power to strengthen, enlighten, enlarge, confirm, and disturb us.

It will be clear that I believe preaching should be biblical. But I do not want this to be understood in too narrow a sense. It does not mean the invariable use of a text. Texts have rather gone out of fashion. Certainly there is no point in quoting one if it is not to be preached upon; mercifully we are delivered from the convention of former years which insisted that sermons should begin in this way. But texts are not to be dismissed; if people remember the sentence or phrase so used, they have something to "take away" with them, and the application may be more readily fixed in the mind. But there are other forms of biblical preaching; the sermon can be based upon a whole story, or a single word, or a personality, or a recurring theme.

Of course there are preachers who think they are expounding the Scriptures when they are in fact airing their own opinions or prejudices. And, of course, it is possible to preach a biblical sermon without using biblical words or illustrations. Preachers are as much subject to human frailty as anyone else. Truth is conveyed through personality, and, conversely, the person can also obscure or obstruct truth. God has always taken risks in the ways in which he communicates with men and women, and he continues to take them. There is never a guarantee that the "pure word of God" will be either preached or heard. But the best hope for the sermon is when preachers retain a high sense of their responsibility as ministers of the Word of God, and congregations have high expectations of hearing that Word.

This chapter has referred to subjects of Christian concern which lie outside the normal range of the sermon. But in many churches, anything outside regular Sunday worship will be attended only by a fraction of the congregation – whether it be a weekday meeting, or even coffee after the service. If the treasurer needs to speak about giving, if a change in liturgy is proposed, if some new area of social concern is to be suggested – all these things may have to be done at the Sunday service. In such cases, confusion is avoided if these important talks are not equated with the sermon. They can be given a different slot in the service, and a brief sermon (three or four minutes) preached after the readings. The Word can be broken in a very short time – this simply requires a different skill from the preacher. But the sermon will retain its importance and its power if it is defined fairly narrowly, and distinguished from other forms of Christian communication – which are not necessarily inferior, but simply different.

THE OPEN BIBLE

In his commentary on St Luke's Gospel, George Caird[6] spoke of its "exquisite Nativity story" as "compounded of three ingredients, prophecy, history and symbolism". The emphasis in this chapter on the Scriptures is not meant to encourage a narrow or uncritical attitude to them. Growth comes from understanding some of the complexities of the Bible, from appreciating the variety as well as the excellence of the Scriptures, from learning more about their background and setting, from assimilating some of the insights of scholars. There ought not to be a chasm between academic and popular theology, and devotion to the Scriptures ought not to be the characteristic only of certain traditions of Christians. To the open Bible we must come with open minds.

Questions

1. Should local churches have their own lectionaries?

2. How can study of the Scriptures be encouraged in your congregation?

3. What do you expect of the sermon?

Notes

1. See *Celebrating Common Prayer* (SSF), and its companion volume *Something Understood* (Hodder & Stoughton).

2. *Patterns for Worship* (Church House Publishing, 1989).

3. The rationale of this is explained in *The Revised Common Lectionary* (Canterbury Press, 1992).

4. *Patterns for Worship*, op cit, p. 14.

5. Donald Coggan, *Stewards of Grace* (Hodder & Stoughton, 1958).

6. George B. Caird, *The Gospel of St Luke* (Pelican, 1963).

3 THE SACRAMENTS

The sacraments are an embodiment of the Word. In the Church of Scotland, Holy Communion has sometimes been called "the action". This refers to what our Lord "did" at the Last Supper, and suggests movement in the service now. In an age which relies so much on the visual, it is not surprising that there has been renewal of sacramental worship and symbolic elements within it. And in most branches of the Christian Church, baptism and the Eucharist are recognized as sacraments, and practised in the course of worship.

CHRISTIAN INITIATION: ITS QUESTIONS

In recent years, the word "initiation" has been used for the whole process by which people are brought into membership of the Church. In many parts of the Church, the traditional process has been infant baptism, instruction throughout childhood, and confirmation (or some parallel service of recognition). In others, infants are dedicated, instruction continues throughout childhood, and baptism follows profession of faith. The line between the two styles of initiation has become rather blurred. The United Reformed Church, by its very composition, practises both "infant" and "believers" baptism. The ASB provides services of thanksgiving for the birth (or adoption) of a child within the initiation section. In churches where infant baptism is the norm, there are parents who believe that it should be deferred. Conversely, some who come to faith in maturity, feel that they were "cheated" by being baptized as infants.[1]

The whole matter of initiation has been the subject of many books and considerable debate in the second half of the twentieth century. Some issues have been particularly acute for the Church of England because its position as the Established Church has meant that many people who seldom attend worship still believe that they have claims upon its ministry. So debate continues about infant baptism. Should it be available to all who ask for it – as a sign of the priority of God's grace, and an affirmation of his accepting love? But can the baptism of infants be justified without some assurance of a specific Christian upbringing? And how real is such assurance if the parents show no sign of worshipping in church or "belonging" to it? Although the question is most acute for Anglicans, it is not unknown in other parts of the Church. Folk religion still seems to be affected by those rubrics of the Prayer Book which stressed the urgency of baptism (the first or second Sunday after birth) and which laid down that the burial service could not be used for the unbaptized. Very few clergy believe that there can be no future beyond the grave for unbaptized children (or adults), and the rubric on emergency baptism in the ASB runs as follows.

> *The parents are responsible for requesting emergency baptism for an infant. They should be assured that questions of ultimate salvation or the provision of a Christian funeral for an infant who dies do not depend upon whether or not he/she has been baptized.*

But the strangers who ring up the vicar to ask if the baby can be "done" have not generally read the rubrics of the ASB!

A second question that is being discussed, and not only by Anglicans, is whether children who have been baptized should be admitted to Holy Communion before they are confirmed. There seem to be two reasons why this is now raised. First there has been the enormous influence of a book published in the middle of the twentieth century – *The Seal of the Spirit*[2] by G. W. H. Lampe – which seemed to establish the completeness of baptism for membership of the Church. Secondly, the fact that the Eucharist is now celebrated in most parts of the Church as a "main" service (rather than one held at an early hour or as an adjunct to regular worship) means that children are often present, and raises the question of their full participation.

The third question has already been briefly suggested. We can put it in personal terms. John and Mary have been brought to faith through a renewal movement. John was never baptized, but did belong to a Baptist youth club. It is now natural for him to undergo total immersion at a Baptist service, and all that seems in accordance with New Testament practice. Mary was baptized in infancy. She has had a conventional Anglican background, but her new experience is quite different. Her vicar says that baptism cannot be repeated, and she can only be baptized with John (which is what she wants) if she denies what once was done for her. What kind of service or ceremony would:

- preserve the unrepeatable nature of baptism, but

- provide Mary with an opportunity of making a public profession of faith and commitment?

CHRISTIAN INITIATION: ITS OPPORTUNITIES

It is time to turn from the problems surrounding Christian initiation to the opportunities it presents for real growth among Christian people. A valuable resource is the report *Baptism Eucharist and Ministry*[3] produced by the Faith and Order Commission of the World Council of Churches after its conference in Lima, Peru, in 1982, and the four principles outlined below have some dependence on that report.

Pluriformity of practice

The Church of the future is bound to include both the baptism of infants and that of believers. "Adult" baptism is now a common and sometimes frequent occurrence in churches where infant baptism remains the norm. Despite what was written earlier, the demand for infant baptism is decreasing in a secular society, and there will always be those whose parents, for a variety of reasons, did not have their children baptized. But it is unlikely that churches practising infant baptism will relinquish the custom, and even more unlikely that churches holding to believers' baptism will start baptizing infants. The Lima report asks for recognition of the once-and-for-all nature of baptism by all branches of the Church and, if this were achieved, it would be a major advance in ecumenical relations. It would more readily commend itself if the remaining three principles were observed.

The solemnity of the occasion

Whatever may be the occasion of baptism, and whatever may be the age of the candidates, the solemnity and importance of the occasion must always be apparent. This does not mean that the service must be stiff and formal, or devoid of the warmth and welcome that should attend it. It does mean that it should never be trivialized. Three ways of emphasizing its importance may be suggested.

1. It is desirable, whenever possible, that baptism should be administered in the course of normal public worship. For Anglicans, this was the intention of the BCP, and is reiterated in

the ASB. In most churches, it is the recommended practice, and one that has been increasingly observed in the last few years. There may be compelling and personal reasons why on some occasions a baptism cannot be conducted in this way, but if it has to be at some different time, the presence of representatives of the worshipping community should be secured. Of its very nature, baptism cannot simply be "a family affair".

2. There must be some way of emphasizing the dimension of water, with all the symbolism suggested by it. In his valuable book *Only Connect,*[4] Robin Green says "There is something in the symbolism of water that both threatens and promises". Certainly, a study of water in the Bible reveals ambiguity, and Robin Green suggests that it should be explored in preparation for baptism.

    At the service itself, water must be more than "sprinkled" if this dimension is to be appreciated. For adults, total immersion needs seriously to be considered. The shape of fonts in Anglican churches suggests the same policy for babies strong enough to stand it, but a proper and visible pouring of water is the least that should be permitted.

3. Alongside this, there must be careful consultation about the place in the church building for baptism, and the provision of sufficient space so that the symbolism and dignity of what is to happen may be perceived. Baptismal cards must be aesthetically worthy. The lighted candle is helpful, but some explanation is needed if it is to be more than a "pretty" adjunct. What is sung on this occasion needs to be different from what might be sung at any service on any Sunday. Two recent hymn books have excellent sections on baptism.[5]

The place of nurture

As we have seen, infant baptism presupposes Christian nurture which will lead to confirmation in which the baptized affirm the promises made on their behalf, and, in some traditions, make others regarding their participation in the life and witness of the Church. But neither confirmation nor believers' baptism ought to be regarded as the end of a process. Most people need some form of nurture beyond that which is provided in the regular worship of the Church. Baptism needs always to be seen in the context of a Church that is committed to growth in understanding and discipleship.

The regularity of renewal

Baptism needs constantly to be renewed. There are a number of ways in which this can happen.

- Every service in which baptism is administered should be seen as an opportunity of reaffirmation by all present. That was one reason why the BCP recommended that it should take place in the context of public worship. The congregation on such occasions is more than a collection of benevolent (if sometimes reluctant) onlookers. They are themselves reminded of their own baptism, and of the privileges and responsibilities that it conferred upon them.

- There are particular occasions for the renewal of baptismal vows. The most obvious of these is confirmation. In the Church of England, candidates make for themselves precisely the same promises that were once made on their behalf. In the United Reformed Church and in the Church of Scotland, they make additional promises about such matters as worship, service, and giving. If the Church of England were to regard confirmation as more than admission to communion, it would need to reconsider what is asked of candidates.

  The formal renewal of baptismal vows has become an annual part of worship in many churches. An increasing number of Anglican churches have an Easter Vigil at which this takes place. *The Promise of His Glory*[6] suggests this possibility at the beginning of the civil year, but offers as an alternative part of the Methodist Covenant service – traditionally used in Methodism on the first Sunday of the New Year, but sometimes on another occasion. As we saw earlier, there is a need for services in which individual Christians could publicly reaffirm their baptism and commitment to Christ.

- The regular worship of the church can provide further opportunities. The Joint Liturgical Group was responsible for appointing a Sunday for the commemoration of Christ's baptism – so long and so strangely neglected in the Western Church. "The life of the baptized" is also a Sunday theme in the present lectionaries derived from the work of the Joint Liturgical Group.

All this can affect the devotional life of Christian people, and ensure that the remembrance of baptism and its implications becomes more central for them. As is well known, Martin Luther at times of great doubt and temptation, would write two words on his table *Baptizatus sum* (I have been baptized). The English Tractarians spoke of "making use of their baptism". To make use of it is a means of growth for us all.

THE EUCHARIST: RENEWED

The sacrament of unity was for many centuries the focus of division among Christians. Two of the Reformation controversies concerned the meaning of Christ's presence at Holy Communion, and the sense in which the language of sacrifice could be applied to that service. At the beginning of the twentieth century, a great gulf seemed fixed between the style of the service in an Anglo-Catholic church, and its style in a Congregational chapel. Within the Church of England itself, controversy had arisen with the Oxford movement in the nineteeth century and, as late as the Second World War, there seemed no way of devising a liturgy that would be acceptable to the parties or schools of thought within it.

The extent to which we have all moved in less than half a century is therefore remarkable, even dramatic. There are signs that the Eucharist is again becoming the sacrament of unity. The ecumenical movement has opened Christians to treasures not their own. The common study of Christian origins by theological students has led them to a reappraisal of their own churchmanship, and led them to evaluate their own practices in the light of deeper and wider historical understanding. This has resulted in three ways of convergence.

Doctrine

Understanding of the biblical concepts of memorial and remembrance has shown that some of the old controversies flourished through ignorance and misunderstanding – sometimes of what words actually meant. Because religious language is often emotive, differences of emphasis and interpretation remain, but it is fair to say that the heat has been taken out of the controversy over the eucharistic sacrifice. The Anglican-Roman Catholic International

Commission[7] report is an outstanding example of this. As to what is meant by the presence of Christ in the Eucharist, there has been a growing recognition of our inability to define this too precisely, and therefore of our unwillingness to try to do so. Again, the Lima report provides a useful description of and commentary upon how far our pilgrimage towards understanding has gone.

Liturgy

Perhaps the greatest milestone in our progress towards liturgical unity was the publication in the 1950s of the eucharistic liturgy of the Church of South India (CSI). This showed that it was possible for those who had been Anglicans, Methodists, Presbyterians, and Congregationalists not only to arrive at a common form of worship, but also to perceive new insights in the process.

The shape of the CSI service, its provision of alternatives and increased lay participation has affected the revisions made in all the mainstream churches in Britain, so that the similarities in their structure and content are more striking than the differences. In this we must include the present form of the Mass in the Roman Catholic Church.

Practice

There has also been increasing agreement that the "normal" Sunday service includes both the reading and preaching of the Word, and the celebration of the Sacrament. For a variety of reasons, this is not the invariable practice in every church. But the service books of the churches are designed with this norm in mind. With the Roman Catholic Church, a sermon or homily is obligatory in every Sunday Mass. In the Church of England, a weekly "parish communion" is held in a large number, probably in the majority, of churches, and there can be very few in which this style of worship is held less than once a month. In the Free Churches, the Communion is now usually celebrated in the course of regular worship, and is much less often treated as something to which a few "stay behind".

I do not want to paint too rosy a picture, or to suggest that our ecumenical problems are solved. Manifestly, they are not. The Roman Catholic Church may not normally receive to Communion those who are outside its number. The presence of women priests creates eucharistic and other divergence within the Church of England. The Salvation Army and the Society of Friends do not observe these sacraments. But these considerations do not minimize the real achievement that has been made in eucharistic understanding and practice.

THE EUCHARIST: MEANS OF RENEWAL

Yet the very high profile given to the Eucharist is not without its problems. There are many within the Church of England who find that their parishes provide no act of worship at which the enquirer or the uncommitted can easily take part. Some are opposed to what has been called "Communion with everything" – including services like inductions to which people are invited because of the positions they hold in the community. Allied to this is the fear that over-frequent Communion may lead to a cheapening of its solemnity and its demands. This fear has been expressed over the weekly Eucharist. The first of these fears lies outside the scope of this chapter. The second clearly belongs to it. It would be impertinent for me to comment further on the frequency of the Eucharist – much less to suggest how often people should be encouraged to attend it. My concern here is with the way in which we can meet the danger of staleness or sameness in its celebration.

The service is, in fact, kaleidoscopic in its meanings, and, because of this, can provide us with a variety of insights and experiences. Some part of this variety is illustrated in the various titles that are given to the service. So far, we have mainly used the word *Eucharist* which is not only the term employed by theologians, but the one which seems most ecumenically accept-able. Eucharist concentrates on the phrase "he gave thanks"; it reminds us that we are responding thankfully to all God's marvellous works – in creation, in redemption, in the present activity of the Holy Spirit. It tells us that the service should never be without joy. Then there is the title *Holy Communion* which reminds us that as we feed on the body and blood of Christ, so we are united with him and with all his people; this term focuses on the Peace, on the intercession, and on what we do at the Table itself. *The Lord's Supper* anchors the celebration in history; it emphasizes the Upper Room, Gethsemane and Calvary, makes these places become the places where we are now, helps us remember the cost of our privileges. The *Mass* is derived from the "dismissal" and reminds us of one of the main insights of modern liturgy, namely the relationship between sacrament and service, between the worship of God in his house, and the worship of God at home, at work, and in human relationships.

These titles are by no means exhaustive, and we need one that suggests we are looking forward to the consummation of the kingdom – which was so marked a feature of early liturgies. But it might be helpful for worshippers to concentrate on just one of the many titles at any one celebration, and then by the use of these and others, to learn the many-sidedness of the celebration in which they are involved.

This can be one way in which we experience growth. Another is provided by different styles of celebration. The Sunday Eucharist in Gloucester Cathedral is accompanied by splendid music and dignified ritual. But on Maundy Thursday evening, a congregation of some 70 people forms a large circle in the spacious Lady Chapel, and gathers around a simple table. Many of those who attend say that this adds a new dimension to their understanding of the Eucharist. In the same cathedral, there are several chapels, furnished in nineteenth-century Tractarian style with the altar against the wall, and the priest with his back to the people. In recent years, one of these has been reordered for a different style of celebration. The table is central, and the seating is arranged around it.

There is not one valid style of celebrating the Eucharist, and many people find themselves enlarged by experiencing a variety of them. You may go up to the altar rails, and receive the elements kneeling, or they may be brought to you as you sit in the pews. You may kneel in "tables", each one receiving a text or blessing, or you may stand in a circle, receiving the elements from your neighbour. Standing, sitting, moving, kneeling – all these postures can make their various contributions to our perception of the Sacrament. So indeed can its setting – in a large church with incense, candles, and colour, or around a small table in a sick person's bedroom, or in the course of a house group in a sitting room. For regular use, many people prefer one style of celebration to another, but one is not "better" than another. Real growth can come when we regularly experience more than one way.

It is good for us all to worship sometimes in other churches, and with different groups of Christians. But some variety in style can be achieved in our own churches. Let me give an Anglican example. In some parishes where the Eucharist is the norm on

Sunday mornings, it has been thought expedient – for reasons of outreach and pastoral concern – to have in its place on one Sunday in the month a non-sacramental "family service". In some such cases, the Eucharist is then celebrated in the evening. Often this will mean a much smaller congregation, and this could provide an opportunity for a different style of celebration – perhaps with more silence, more meditation, simpler music, greater spontaneity, and maybe a different approach to the sermon. Care could be taken in choosing the part of the church to be used for such a service.

We must not neglect the necessity for imagination and care in planning "normal" worship. Flexibility within given structures is one of the liturgical axioms of our day, and within that structure there is certainly room for variety in music, in ways of prayer, and in styles of preaching. Some Anglicans were once suspicious of more than one eucharistic prayer; but in the future they may have even more than four. Of course there is need for stability as well as variety, and the balancing of these needs will be examined in Chapter 7.

What has been written above may give the impression that every Eucharist ought to provide fresh novelty and new excitement. Of course this is not so. In the famous classic *The Shape of the Liturgy*,[8] Dom Gregory Dix said of the Eucharist in the fourth century that the service was "bare and unimpressive to the point of dullness". So it has been for Christians in many centuries and in many places, yet they have been nourished and strengthened by it. Nor are we to suppose that we can systematically chart our spiritual progress or evaluate our spiritual growth. As with plants, much growth is under the soil. Christians are called to meet their Lord, and their brothers and sisters in the Faith, even when it does not seem to mean much, and when it affords little spiritual glow. Experiences and feelings are gifts, not rights.

It is the many-sidedness of the Eucharist that enables us to grow in our perception of its meaning. Such a perception is not a once-and-for-all gift, and participation in this service is not the prerogative of those who have "arrived". John Wesley spoke of it as "a converting ordinance", and it is one which always brings us back to the central things – to what God has done in Christ, and continues to do through his Holy Spirit in us. P. T. Forsyth wrote:

> *When you reflect after Communion "What have I done today?", say to yourself "I have done more than on any busiest day of the week. I have yielded myself to take part with the Church in Christ's finished Act of Redemption, which is greater than the making of the world".[9]*

Questions

1. How far does the way in which you celebrate the Eucharist in your church reflect its meanings?

2. Where should the baptistery be sited, and what should it look like?

3. Discuss John Wesley's claim that the Eucharist is "a converting ordinance".

Notes

1. Many of these questions are addressed in the Anglican report *On the Way: Towards an Integrated Approach to Christian Initiation* (Church House Publishing, 1995) which appeared shortly before this book was being prepared for publication.

2. Geoffrey W. H. Lampe, *The Seal of the Spirit* (SPCK, 1967).

3. *Baptism, Eucharist and Ministry* (WCC, 1982).

4. Robin Green, *Only Connect* (Darton, Longman and Todd, 1987).

5. *Hymns and Psalms* (Methodist Publishing House, 1983); and *Rejoice and Sing* (Oxford University Press, 1991).

6. *The Promise of His Glory* (Church House Publishing and Mowbrays, 1991).

7. The Anglican-Roman Catholic International Commission published the Agreed Windsor Statement on Eucharistic Doctrine, 1971.

8. Gregory Dix, *The Shape of the Liturgy* (Dacre/Black, 1945).

9. Quoted in J. A. T. Robinson, *Liturgy Coming to Life* (Mowbrays, 1960), p. 109.

4 RITES OF PASSAGE

During the twentieth century, and doubtless sometimes in others, weddings and funerals have been the only times that many people have entered a church building to take part in an act of worship. When people have no connection at all with any church, it is likely that their funerals will take place in a crematorium (or cemetery) chapel. In the case of weddings, the choice, until now, has been between the register office and a place for worship licensed for the purpose. It remains to be seen whether the new facility for weddings to take place at other sites will be widely used.

CHURCH WEDDINGS

Weddings can be a source of much irritation to local church communities. They often feel that their buildings are being taken over by people who have scant regard for what they stand for, and whose contribution to their maintenance (through the standard fees) is fairly minimal. One local newspaper often reports that such-and-such a church was the "setting for the wedding of…" and this says a lot. A priest who had spent most of his ministry in a non-parochial situation was a few years ago temporarily in charge of a group of parishes in the north, and he described weddings as "a more or less equal mixture of the Chelsea Flower Show, Trooping the Colour, the Miss World Competition and a film company on location".[1] Sometimes it does seem, even in a church wedding, that the actual service comes low on the list of priorities – both in expenditure and attention.

But it is not possible to estimate the degree of sincerity about Christian marriage in those who are about to take part in it, and, indeed, no one should try to do so. As with infant baptism, there may be a vague and inarticulate reaching out to the spiritual realm. Many ministers who take trouble over marriage preparation have realized this, and sought patiently and sensitively to develop any signs of spiritual awareness. At weddings, as in all rites of passage, it is only too easy to break the bruised reed and to quench the smouldering wick.

A rubric before the ASB Marriage Service runs:

> *... prayers which the couple have written or selected in co-operation with the priest may be used. Silence may be kept; or free prayer may be offered.*

Long before the ASB was devised, it was, of course, common for the BCP service to be supplemented with additional material. A diocesan pastoral regulation of the 1950s told the clergy "the Bishop does not discourage the use of alternative prayers in the marriage and funeral services". Doubtless all this was normal in those churches not committed to uniformity in worship.

But the ASB rubric, together with the options built into the service itself (most of which are mirrored in the service books of many parts of the Christian Church), does mean that the couple who are to be married can play a large part in the construction of the service which is to celebrate their wedding. No longer need the minister "go through" the service with them, merely asking what hymns they would like. The new liturgical freedom provides very considerable pastoral opportunities. If they are to be exploited to the full, it is essential that "preparation" should begin as early as possible. Many couples who opt for a church wedding come to it with a lot of preconceived ideas, and even regular worshippers can be mistaken about what a church wedding entails. For example, people sometimes say that they have decided to have their wedding in a register office because they want it to be very quiet and simple, and they have not realized that a wedding in church can be both of these things. Bridesmaids, flowers, and music are not essential ingredients of a marriage service. Every part of the Christian Church has its own discipline about what should be said and done, and when the minister acts as registrar, the service must reflect what is required by the law of the land. But all that still leaves considerable freedom in the content of the service. During the time of preparation, people often need gently to move from saying what "I like" to what is appropriate for their wedding. The questions to be asked are "What do you want to express/affirm/celebrate at your wedding?"

In 1986, the Canterbury Press produced, for use in cemeteries and crematoria, a book containing the funeral services of the main branches of the church in England, and Kenneth Stevenson[2] has suggested that a similar publication for marriage would be of great value. Again it could contain the official services of the mainstream churches, together with a selection of prayers, readings, and hymns. Such an ecumenical collection would bring the insights of the various denominations within the reach of all. We might still want to choose material not contained within its covers, and we might still want to press for a more adequate revision of the service in our own tradition, but our thinking might be very much helped by such a publication.

When a wedding takes place in a church, it must be of some concern to those who worship there. Obviously, this will be expressed when the couple are themselves worshippers, though the weddings of non-churchgoers could be marked by some token of care and acceptance by the church community. Kenneth Stevenson has suggested that the marriage rites could be spread over a longer period than is usual. The "betrothal" or engagement could be affirmed liturgically as well as by a secular party. From then on, prayers would be regularly offered for those preparing for marriage (this happens in many churches when the banns are called). Perhaps in some cases the marriage celebration could take place in the course of Sunday worship, or be closely related to it. All this might more effectively reflect the stages through which people pass in "rites of passage" and give a deeper context to the marriage. Many pastors would argue that over-emphasis on the wedding day itself has an adverse effect on our understanding of marriage, and so on marriages themselves.

CHRISTIAN FUNERALS

Many a novel published in the twentieth century has begun with a funeral – often portrayed as cold and formal, and strangely inappropriate to the deceased. Similarly, stories abound of funerals conducted perfunctorily or insensitively, and even of clergy who got the sex of the dead person wrong.

Clergy and ministers may often be culpable, but two things must be said in their defence. First, they have been called upon to conduct funerals of people almost or totally unknown to them. This has certainly happened to those on cemetery or crematorium duty. Secondly, the funeral services of most churches presuppose faith in those present, and assume it of the departed. Such services speak of the hope of resurrection, the reality of judgement, and the comfort of the Scriptures. Until recently, not many people have realized that there are alternatives to the Christian funeral service, but it remains the easier option. The secular funeral is now a real possibility, but it requires as much thought, care, and discussion as there ought to be in the arrangement of a Christian funeral. So many who do not feel that they can cope with that opt for the service as set out in the booklets provided in crematorium or cemetery chapels.

Attention has been given in recent years by many branches of the Church – notably the Roman Catholics – to their funeral rites. But some of us still want to ask questions about what we are doing at a funeral. Such questions were asked by the Anglican Liturgical Commission in 1965, and they arrived at certain theological answers and some practical consequences.[3] But areas which seem to need some attention are as follows.

The recognition of death and mortality

This ought to be obvious in the presence of the coffin, but sometimes tends to be smoothed over. A famous sermon by Bernard Lord Manning, Cambridge historian and lay preacher, and recently described as "Catholic Calvinist", strongly defended the use of Psalm 90 (rather than 23 or 121) on the grounds that we cannot receive the gospel of the resurrection until we have faced up to our own mortality.

The place of grief and guilt

Many orders of service give the impression that grief is inappropriate, and that it contradicts the faith that Christians hold. This is surely untrue – theologically and psychologically. And it needs to be expressed together with guilt. Few do so, but the URC service book 1989 has an opening prayer which runs:

> *God of life and love, we come to you in our need. Be with us as we experience the abyss of death and grief. Be there in our sorrow and pain; be with us in our fear, that we may find light in darkness and comfort in your Word.*

And later there is a prayer:

> *Help us confess any hurt, and wrong we feel that we have done to…, and help us to know that we are forgiven as we hear your words "Those who come to me, I will not cast out".[4]*

The "personalized" funeral

The need for the funeral service to be in some way related to the character and interests of the dead person is being increasingly realized. This is very difficult unless there is a meeting between the officiant and the bereaved family, and is not easily achieved through the offices of undertakers, however caring and sensitive they may be. It is now very common for an address to be given at a funeral, and neither honesty nor humour are out of place in it. As with weddings, there can be a wide selection of prayers and music, though care needs to be taken over their suitability, and perhaps reference to the selection made in the address.

The leave-taking

It was customary at burials for the mourners to file past the grave and look in – perhaps dropping a flower or casting earth. There seems no parallel procedure in the case of cremations, although various possibilities have been suggested. Recent service books have suggested that where the service takes place in church, it concludes with a commendation of the dead person, and that is the leave-taking; what follows then becomes an appendix to a service that is already complete. But perhaps this leave-taking needs to be more than a form of words uttered by the minister, and there is room for consideration of how this might be accompanied by some simple ritual. Pastors have often supposed that funeral services are primarily for the comfort of the living, but recent studies have shown the need of the bereaved for some specific form of leave-taking, and that the actual dispatch of the body is for them the primary purpose of the service.

What has been written above is in no way intended to minimize the other elements in the service – the proclamation of the resurrection-hope, the affirmation of God's love and care for all that he has made, the comfort and strength which come from his promises in the Scriptures, and the need for all taking part to be reminded of the brevity and value of life. On this last point the mandatory prayer of the ASB is surely one of its most valuable parts:

Grant us, Lord, the wisdom and the grace to use aright the time that is left to us here on earth. Lead us to repent of our sins, the evil we have done and the good we have not done; and strengthen us to follow the steps of your Son, in the way that leads to the fullness of eternal life.

But what the ASB and other service books do very well must be taken alongside what seems to be missing or submerged in them, and that is the reason for the considerations advanced in previous paragraphs.

As with weddings, this book must ask how funerals affect the life of a local church. Where the dead person was a worshipper, the answer is as straightforward as it was for weddings. But the process of secularization has, together with modern funeral customs, resulted in a distancing of people from the place of worship with which they might have felt some contact. It was common in Anglican and Roman Catholic churches for the body to be brought to church on the day before a funeral and "rested" there overnight. Again, it was, until recently, common in many denominations for the mourners to attend church in a body on the following Sunday, and in the north of England, this was sometimes known as the memorial service. They were sometimes invited to choose a hymn, which meant that congregations might find themselves singing "Abide with me" every Sunday evening. Today it would probably be "The day thou gavest" (not very suitable in the morning) or "The old rugged cross" (not very suitable at any time). But perhaps the custom should be revived in some form. Or there might be an annual service of remembrance such as *The Promise of His Glory* suggests for All Saints-tide. The use of churchyards or church grounds for the burial of cremated remains can be a link with the local church – though care must be taken not to make such areas look like mini-cemeteries.

And worship as a whole needs to capture that vivid sense of the communion of saints that has often been lacking in the West. It is not the function of the Church to give easy, cheap answers about death; we ourselves are in the presence of a mystery which we struggle to comprehend. There is a time for silence as well as for words. But neither death nor the departed should ever be ignored.

BIRTH, SICKNESS, BEREAVEMENT

Hospital chaplains are among those who have drawn the attention of the churches to the pastoral need of a liturgy for use at the birth of a stillborn child, and the death of a newly-born child. The ASB in 1980 provided a selection of prayers for such times, and produced in 1989 a funeral service for a child dying near the time of birth.[5] This was preceded by an introduction which sought to face the theological questions raised by such services, as well as the pastoral needs to which they were addressed.

The whole area of ministry to the sick was not much represented in the ASB, but a supplementary booklet appeared three years later.[6] This included arrangements for communion, laying on of hands, and anointing together with prayers for use with the sick, and a commendation at the time of death. There are now churches of many traditions which regularly hold healing services. These may be on a Sunday at the time of regular worship, or that worship may include the laying on of hands – perhaps at the end of the communion. Other churches have such services on a weekday, sometimes on a monthly basis. Both the URC and Baptist service books provide outlines and material for such services, together with introductions which explore the nature of Christian healing and seek to remove misconceptions. This provision is likely to be made by other churches when revising their service books, but in the mean time the two mentioned above provide very useful resource material.

The growth of hospices has meant a rather different approach than has been common for much of the twentieth century, and in response to those involved in this ministry, the Liturgical Commission has produced *Ministry at the Time of Death,*[7] which enlarges on its earlier provision for the sick. The booklet includes a form for anointing before death. Unction has not been generally practised among Anglicans, and has been little known in the Free Churches, but the URC book draws attention to this possibility.

HUMAN SEXUALITY

The prevalence of divorce and remarriage has created problems with which the churches have wrestled in the twentieth century, and there are probably no church communities and few families unaffected by it. The problem is how to balance the Christian affirmation of life-long marriage with the pastoral needs of those whose marriage has broken down, how to witness both to Christian moral standards and to the principle of redemption which lies at the heart of the Christian faith. The attitude of the Roman Catholic Church is uncompromising and well known. Free Church ministers, on the whole, have, in certain circumstances, shown themselves willing to conduct the weddings of those whose previous marriages have been dissolved, but the Methodist and URC service books also contain forms of service that may be used after civil marriages. The Church of England has not been able to arrive at a conclusion on the matter. By law, a member of the clergy may officiate at such a wedding. Diocesan regulations have strongly dissuaded clergy from doing so, but there has been a more relaxed attitude in recent years. Forms of "blessing" have been authorized in many dioceses, but in 1985 the Liturgical Commission produced a pamphlet which (significantly?) omitted the word "blessing" and used the title "Services of Prayer and Dedication After a Civil Marriage".[8]

It would not be appropriate here to summarize the debate which has led to the present situation, or to discuss the anomalies that are represented within it. Suffice it to say that most churches outside the Roman Communion recognize the possibility of another union after a marriage breakdown, and are prepared to call it marriage. There are those who would argue for the continental practice in which all marriages take place in the presence of a registrar. This would, perhaps, give even greater freedom to the construction of the ensuing church service, and thus contribute to the growth in faith and discipleship of those who have asked for it.

There are far more controversial issues in this area. A few years ago, SPCK decided not to publish what was then called a book of "gay" services. Another publisher did so, and the matter continues to be debated.[9] The appropriateness of such prayers and services must depend, in the first instance, on whether or not Christians regard homosexual relationships as "sinful". If they do not, and if they regard acceptance of such relationships as desirable, they will want to do something to encourage their stability, and this will call for some public and liturgical affirmation.

The groups who discuss this chapter may want to ask the basic question "What, now, is living in sin?" If their answers are different from what has been the traditional response to such a question, they will want to ask further what can be affirmed by a Christian community, and what liturgical expressions such affirmations involve.

OTHER "PASSAGES" IN LIFE

The final section of this chapter calls for considerable exploration by those who read and discuss it. Are there other transitions in life that call for some liturgical expression – of thanksgiving, commendation, or dedication? Retirement could be an example of these. It involves a change in lifestyle that could be as great as that involved in marriage. How it is to be understood will depend upon whether it is "normal", early or compulsory, but it does mean a new way of life, and perhaps that should be marked in church.

At the other end of life, there is need for the Christian community to remember in prayer those who are starting work or taking on a new job with great responsibility. The Episcopal Prayer Book of the USA has a form of commitment to Christian service which could be included in any act of worship. The URC book has a form of commissioning of church-related community workers. But might there not be commissioning of Christian people whose social or community work is going to be done in an entirely secular setting?

In recent years, there has been great interest in what is called "Celtic spirituality". Part of its appeal lies in the integration of the Christian faith with the created order, and of our own religious practice with the actual lives that we live. If this affects the spirituality of individual Christians, it will have a spin-off in the worship of the church. Of course there is the danger that the natural order will be seen as an escape from the industrialized society in which most of us find ourselves in these islands. Yet it is vitally important that the ordinary concerns of life should be reflected in our worship, and that what happens on Sundays should be related to what happens in the rest of the week. The very term "Celtic spirituality" suggests that this is hardly a new insight, but one to which the Church has been recalled again and again in its history, and through a number of movements in the twentieth century. It is for this reason that this chapter on "rites of passage" has touched on a number of matters not normally associated with that term.

But not all will want their personal lives directly mentioned in the worship of the church to which they belong. There are some people who do not want their names to be put on prayer lists when they are ill. This is not necessarily culpable, and a certain reticence about oneself is not inconsistent with full participation in the life of the church.

> *I know not, O I know not*
> *What social joys are there*

sang Bernard of Cluny. It is doubtless well that we do not know. And many of us hope that even those social joys will be various.

Questions

1. What changes would you like to see in the marriage/funeral services of your church?

2. What relationships can be blessed in church, and in what way?

3. Are there any other stages in life that need some liturgical expression?

Notes

1. Contribution by Kenneth Stevenson in Michael Perham (ed.), *Liturgy for a New Century* (SPCK/Alcuin, 1991).

2. *Liturgy for a New Century*, op cit, pp. 58–9.

3. These are quoted in Jasper and Bradshaw, *A Companion to the Alternative Service Book* (SPCK, 1986).

4. *Service Book of the URC* (Oxford University Press, 1989).

5. *Funeral Service for a Child Dying Near the Time of Birth* (Church House Publishing, 1989).

6. *Ministry to the Sick*, 1983.

7. Church House Publishing, as note 5.

8. Church House Publishing, 1985.

9. Elizabeth Stewart (ed.), *Daring to Speak Love's Name* (Hamish Hamilton, 1992).

5 OCCASIONAL SERVICES

It is not easy for the enquirer or uncommitted person to drop in as an observer of Christian worship. Churches are less "open" than they were to strangers – despite, or maybe because of, the notice-boards which proclaim that all are welcome. You cannot slip into the back seat of the gallery in some large chapel, because no one now sits in the gallery; and the same may be true of the aisles in our parish churches. Anglican worship has become increasingly sacramental, and this can seem exclusive to those who are not communicants. Family services can have the same effect on those who are not members of nuclear families. Smaller congregations often suggest tighter membership. Cathedrals or large centres of worship are the only places in which it is comfortable to be some sort of onlooker.

Yet the Church still has – potentially – a large fringe membership. This becomes apparent on such occasions as carol services, Mothering or Remembrance Sunday, a service celebrating the birthday of some organization, or even Songs of Praise in a village church. How such occasions can help those who attend – for a variety of reasons – to grow in understanding and maybe in discipleship is the subject of this chapter.

CAROL SERVICES

Carol services continue to attract large congregations despite the fact that the tunes (and sometimes the words) have been heard for weeks on radio stations, in stores, and in the streets. Gloucester Cathedral is filled twice over on Christmas Eve for services of this kind – and in the previous ten days has similarly been filled by schools and other organizations holding their own carol services. This is true of most of our large centres of worship, but the smallest congregations are likely to find their numbers swelled for the carol service.

The carol service can do little more than provide yet another layer of sentimentality at Christmas. But those of us who are inclined to lament the commercialization of this season ought to reflect a little on its history. This was originally a pagan festival which the Church sought to baptize. It never quite succeeded in doing so, and it seems as if it has almost been recaptured by secular forces. There is a wide chasm between what Christians mean by Christmas, and what most people mean by it. We are wise not to be over-censorious or smug about all this. Most of us enjoy receiving presents and eating our Christmas dinner, and there is no reason why we should not. And we are always more affected than we realize or admit by the standards of the secular world to which we belong.

An absent-minded curate leading the Lord's Prayer at this season once said "Forgive us our Christmases as we forgive those who Christmas against us". We could probably make a long list of those who have Christmased against us! But we need also to be forgiven for our own Christmases. For most of my ministry, I have been more worried by the religious observance of Christmas than by its commercialization.

For it can, as I have said, be no more than a nostalgic and sentimental exercise. The Bible can be read as if it were entirely self-explanatory, and hymns and carols chosen with scant reference to their words – some of which do not stand up to much examination. There are at least two questions to which we should address ourselves in the planning of Christmas worship, and especially in the planning of those services which attract irregular worshippers. First, we must ask what Christ's coming to this world really meant, and secondly what it means to live an incarnational faith in the contemporary world.

In response to these questions, I suggest four areas to which attention should be given in the planning of what we call carol services.

1. There must be a search for biblical passages which illustrate this festival, which place the birth of Jesus in the context of his life, death, resurrection, and ascension, and which place these supreme saving events in the context of God's eternal purpose for this world. This means that we do not confine ourselves to the second chapter of St Luke's Gospel. In fact, few carol services do so; but if, for example, we read from Genesis 3 there needs to be some explanation – either by the reader or on the service paper – of why we do so. In a freer kind of worship, readings from the Bible could well be balanced by the prose and poetry of the Christian centuries, and the biblical passage itself illuminated by

the writings of later ages. But whatever is read must be read well. If there are seven readings, do not look for seven organizations that ought to be represented, but rather for seven good readers. If the two considerations coincide, so much the better. Rehearsals for such readings are never unnecessary.

2. There must be careful scrutiny of the words and music to be used in the carols, hymns, or songs. Besides those which tell the story, there must be those which explore its meaning – such as the great Wesley hymns on the incarnation. There is room for one or two lullabies in the service, but not for half a dozen. If some item like "The holly and the ivy" is to be chosen, we must ask why. It could point in its way to the redemption of the created order, and that would be a good reason for its inclusion. We certainly want some songs that may be less familiar because they seek to explore the *contemporary* meaning of Christmas. When *100 Hymns for Today*[1] was first published, "Every star shall sing a carol" and "No use knocking at the window" sought to do this – perhaps in what now seems an ephemeral and not very satisfactory way. But each generation has to express what all this seems to mean, and the Iona Community has tried to do this in a very striking way.[2]

3. Attention must be given to the visual – to ritual and to movement. Sometimes at this season, carol services are described as being "by candlelight". One wonders why. It can simply provide a pretty background to the service. But the candle remains a powerful religious (and sometimes secular) symbol. It can certainly be over-used in worship, so when it is used we must try to get it right. The question "why" must be asked of most matters under this heading of the visual, and we must do our best to ensure that what people see gives them the right message.

4. There is surely a strong case for some kind of sermon in services of this kind, even if its length corresponds to "Thought for the day". Here is a golden (surely God-given) opportunity to commend the gospel. It will entail a lot of work if it is to be done well and, the shorter the sermon, the more care will be needed for its preparation. Alternatively, each of the readings could be preceded or followed by some exposition or explanation of the passage. There is always the danger that expositions can rob a passage of its meaning, but equally that meaning can be illuminated. It would probably be desirable for all the

introductions to be written and delivered by one person to avoid duplication. These two methods are alternative to each other, as such services should not be heavily didactic, and people should not be made to feel that they are being "got at". The aim is the exposition as well as the proclamation of the gospel.

Many books offer outlines of services and sequences of readings. Generally, these are better regarded as source material for the compilation of worship rather than ready-made liturgies. The framing of a carol service could profitably begin quite early in the autumn with a group of people meeting and asking the basic question "What are we trying to do?" The final compilation could then be in the hands of two or three people who would seek to use the material offered to them so as to maintain balance, structure, and flow in the service that they construct.

Before leaving this subject, it is probably worth saying again that there are several seasons of the year in which this format is suitable. Carols are not confined to Christmas, and one of our older standard collections showed that they were written for many occasions both in the ecclesiastical and in the natural year. Advent carol services have become increasingly popular in recent years; Epiphany, Easter and Pentecost may not draw the crowds, but will provide opportunities of participation in these festivals and certainly of reflection upon them. In *The English Carol*[3] Erik Routley included among his examples a service for Lent on these principles – designed for a college where the members would not be there for Holy Week and Easter. Sequences of music and readings can be devised on a variety of themes – not all of them concerned with the Christian year.

FESTIVALS SACRED AND SECULAR

There are at least three other occasions in the year when festivals or observances have a nationwide appeal and draw more worshippers to our churches. The first of these is Mothering Sunday, when some churches record congregations as large as those at Christmas. This is now very largely a secular observance. Mothering Sunday does indeed have a long history; but present customs go far beyond the relaxation of discipline allowed on a Sunday in the middle of Lent. The day is more commonly described as "Mother's Day" and it focuses on family reunions, or the sending of cards or presents to mothers.

This is laudable enough, but it need not and should not dominate the whole character of worship on this Sunday. But in view of the strains put on family life in our society, it is good to have one day in the year when there is thanksgiving for families and affirmation of their importance. In fact, the calendar adopted some years ago by most of the mainstream churches did appoint such a day on the fourteenth Sunday after Pentecost, and it would be more suitable to have such a celebration in the summer or early autumn than on the Sunday just before the commemoration of the Passion of Our Lord. It would also be good if the occasion involved all the members of the family without diminishing the unique role of mothers. "Father's Day" is advertised on a Sunday in June, but does not seem to have particular liturgical observances in our churches; even if it has, one wants to ask what about brothers and sisters, uncles and aunts, cousins and grandparents, or even child-minders?

But if we are seeking to recover an occasion that has become secular, we are probably left with the fourth Sunday in Lent, and must ask what a special service on that day should include. Certainly and obviously there must be the following.

- Thanksgiving for parents and families and for the special calling of mothers, but surely also:

- prayer for those to whom family life has brought tension and sorrow and hurt. An earlier chapter in this book referred to the current Baptist source book of services which has some very realistic prayers for this occasion. And there needs to be:

- some exposition of the biblical idea of families that is also honest, and tells us more than that they are "a good thing". We must also consider:

- the wider application which might take us to the family of the church, the family of the local community, or even to the whole human family. And the service has to include ritual and movement that have been carefully considered. Some churches provide bunches of flowers for children to give to their mothers, and if the provision has been over-generous, extend the gifts to all the women in the congregation. What exactly does this say?

The whole occasion requires sensitivity and imagination, and it can so easily seem to exclude those who do not enjoy the ideal circumstances the service seems to extol. A group drawing up this service should certainly include both a single person, and a parent who is trying to bring up children alone.

Harvest Thanksgiving services may have declined in popularity as Mothering Sunday services have increased – this often seems to be the case in urban settings. But here we have something even more basic – thanksgiving for daily food and the fruits of the earth. This is another occasion which can easily degenerate into nostalgia for some past Arcady. Many churches do their best to avoid this by having collections for Christian Aid, and suggesting gifts of practical and longer term usefulness than the products of garden and orchard – delightful and welcome as these things are. Harvest Thanksgiving services must not neglect their primary function – which is to give thanks for daily bread. But they must also include such matters as:

- our stewardship of the natural resources and our accountability for their use;

- the Old Testament emphasis that harvest must make provision for the alien and stranger;

- the New Testament use of harvest as a symbol of the work of the Church and the fulfilment of the kingdom of God.

If this happens in sermons and prayers, it must be reflected in the parts of the worship. One way involves consideration of what is *offered* in the service and for what purpose. Another involves the choice of hymns and songs. I began *The Use of Hymns* with a description of a Harvest Thanksgiving service in which none of the hymns made specific response to the word of God as it had been interpreted that day. This is by no means the only occasion in the year where there is crying need for hymnody that will "send us out". Such material may often be found in sections of hymn books that are not directly concerned with harvest. But the closing hymn for this and many occasions presents a challenge to hymn-writers to compose words enabling us to grow in understanding and, in our own way, to serve the present age.

Turning to Remembrance Sunday, the best that I can do in this book is to plead for a new service. The official form now in use was first published as far back as 1968. In 1984 it was slightly modernized, the "you" form for prayers adopted, and a fresh selection of hymns provided. When the Liturgical Commission produced *The Promise of His Glory* the service was reprinted there, but appended to it was an act of thanksgiving that had been curiously absent from the official order. The service is neither nationalistic nor militaristic in tone; some of the ceremonies that surround it may be open to those criticisms, but they do not apply to the service itself. Its main defect is that it is too narrow in its reference, despite the fact that the forms of prayer within it may be expanded. There remains a place for the commemoration of those who died in the service of their country in the two world wars and indeed through the rest of the twentieth century. But this could be widened to include all who have died in the cause of justice and freedom, and there is room for fuller forms of intercession for world peace and dedication to its promotion. The sort of material now used for "One World Week" services that occur just a fortnight earlier might well be used here, and indeed the two occasions might be brought together. And there is similarly a need to reconsider the whole structure of the service.

Of course, churches that do not have an official parade will make their own arrangements for observance of this day, and often that will mean the inclusion of special material within the normal structures of worship. But such churches may not find their congregations especially large on this Sunday. On the other hand, official Remembrance Sunday services do attract large congregations, and, interestingly, they seem in many places to be increasing rather than declining. They will certainly include many people who do not normally go to church, some whose faith is minimal, some who are required to attend because of the positions they hold, or the organizations to which they belong. The occasion provides a great opportunity for setting forth the relevance of the Christian gospel to the world in which we live. Needless to say, the sermon is of great importance on such an occasion. Much care must be exercised in the choice of a preacher, and much care must be exercised by the preacher who is chosen.

More local are civic services or Mayor's Sunday. In some areas, this takes place in a central parish church, but in others it may be held in the place of worship with which the civic leader has a connection. In either case, but certainly in the first, this is an occasion that should be planned ecumenically, specific local needs borne in mind, and many of the considerations mentioned for Remembrance Sunday apply here. In many areas, this also raises the question of multi-faith worship – a much-debated theological issue which lies outside the scope of this book.

The habit of designating certain Sundays for special causes has grown considerably in this century. We have already noted the degeneration of Mothering Sunday into Mother's Day. In recent years "Sea Sunday" has appeared in July, and a national music day was announced on a Sunday in 1992. Admittedly, some observances that flourished earlier in the century have now lapsed – such as Empire/Commonwealth Youth Sunday which used to coincide with the Sunday after Ascension Day. Many of these specially designated Sundays are secular in origin, and may or may not affect the worship of the local church. But some 50 years ago, a clerical wit found himself wondering how soon Christmas would be known as "baby day" and Easter as "egg Sunday".

Within those churches which used to sit more lightly to the ecclesiastical year, there were a whole number of "special" Sundays. Methodists, among others, may remember the time when Sunday School Anniversary services drew large crowds and were often the most popular features of the year. To this could be added Choir Sunday, Guild Anniversary, Women's and Men's Sundays and Church Anniversary; the Anglican counterpart of the last-named was Dedication or Patronal Festival. Such events are now more often low key, and in some cases tie in with the Christian Year – now much more generally observed. Education Sunday, for example, which used to be observed in the autumn, is now linked with the ninth Sunday before Easter which has as its theme "Christ the Teacher". And although the Sunday themes originally devised by the Joint Liturgical Group have become less popular among those who seek to influence our liturgy, they do lend themselves to some of the occasions noted above.

There are still organizations within the Church that want a special service on a particular Sunday, and there are other organizations loosely or scarcely connected with it that want to observe an anniversary or have some emblem dedicated – perhaps outside the normal times of worship, but perhaps within that worship itself. In my book *Special Services for Festivals and Occasions*,[4] I have suggested a very broad outline of how such services might be planned, and offered a check-list of questions that need to be answered before the planning takes place.

In the context of this book, we are concerned with the way in which these services can contribute to the growth of those who participate in them. Although I have been writing about a wide variety of occasions and interests, I think there are certain things that are common to them all. First, the members of these organizations want their organization to be affirmed. There may be some within them who see the need for widespread change, but there will be few who wonder whether the body to which they belong has outlived its usefulness. Secondly, those who ask for these services have some belief in a spiritual dimension to the work in which they are engaged. This may be fairly inarticulate, and may be overlaid with convention and custom, but it is not very fashionable to go to church for anything, and the spiritual quest must always be recognized and encouraged by those who are planning the service.

The representatives of the church community planning these services need sensitivity and tact on the one hand, and clarity and conviction on the other. The Church is not in the business of blessing uncritically all that goes on in the organizations of the secular community, or the organizations within its own community. But again it must not quench the smoking flax. It must meet people where they are, yet help them to move a little way forward, to see worship as an encounter with the living God, and to be open to his word. The pastoral and prophetic work of the Church go together. If we do not move people by an inch, we have failed in our work; if we try to move them two inches at the same time, we may lose them for ever.

SONGS OF PRAISE

Only a few words can be given at this point about what is one of the most popular of special events – Songs of Praise. The effect of this occasion at local level can bear similarity to the BBC programme which has such widespread viewing. In *The Use of Hymns* I suggested some ways in which this occasion might be arranged, and further suggested that it had an important spin-off not only for hymn singing, but for worship in general. It can similarly be important for Christian growth, if it becomes a bit more than a comfortable and undemanding exercise. It can again be a way in which the gospel can seem to speak to our present age. To this we shall return in Chapter 8.

Questions

1. Discuss the rival claims of "special Sundays" and the ordered sequence of the Christian year.

2. How should carol services end?

3. How can a Mothering Sunday service be so planned that it relates to everyone present?

Notes

1. Still published separately, but now included in *Hymns Ancient & Modern* New Standard (Canterbury Press, 1983).

2. See the various volumes of Wild Goose Songs, Iona Community.

3. Erik Routley, *The English Carol* (Jenkins, 1958).

4. Alan Dunstan, *Special Services for Festivals and Occasions* (Kevin Mayhew, 1991).

6 THE PEOPLE AND THE PLACE

BUILDINGS

In a small Cornish fishing village, the Anglicans and Methodists have recently pooled their resources. The village had a little mission church, which in recent years was used for a monthly celebration of Holy Communion. Not far from it was the Methodist chapel, dating from the earlier part of the last century, and having a seating capacity of 150 for a weekly congregation that barely reached double figures. The mission church has been most attractively reordered; a painted screen at the west end conceals the toilet and kitchen that are now indispensable to church premises; well-designed chairs, the colour of the screen, occupy the nave; the chancel has a simple and beautiful free-standing altar, and unobtrusive curtains may be drawn across the chancel when social events take place in the nave. All this has resulted in a definite though undramatic increase in congregations.

This simple and obvious solution for the small worshipping communities was doubtless the result of much heart-searching and discussion. It could be the envy of many, but for a variety of reasons, it is not a scheme that could be invariably repeated. Many Christians today meet in buildings which were designed for a different size of congregation and for a different style of worship. For Anglicans, this is hardly a new situation. The medieval buildings designed for the Mass as it was then celebrated, were not suited to the services of the Prayer Book, and often the churches were divided into two parts. Anglicans had to wait for the architect Sir Christopher Wren in the late seventeeth century before they had purpose-built churches. The nineteenth century saw a return to buildings that were medieval in inspiration, and which suited the liturgical ideas of High Anglicanism, and these are not easily adaptable to the styles of worship that have become popular in the second half of the twentieth century. Diocesan advisory committees for the care of churches have reordering schemes regularly on the agenda for their meetings.

And these are by no means simply Anglican problems. Roman Catholics have, for a slightly longer period, been trying to adapt their churches for celebrations of the Mass in which the priest faces the people. The great Free Churches of the nineteenth century were built on the assumption that the ministry of the Word was paramount, and that everyone present should be able to see and hear the preacher; so, from a lofty pulpit or rostrum, the preacher could survey those in the gallery as well as those on the floor of the house. But such an arrangement loses its point when the gallery is seldom occupied, the main part of the building less than half full, the worship itself more sacramental in character, and there is an expressed desire for more movement and colour in the services.

Hence many worshippers do not find the buildings in which they meet suited to the styles of worship which now prevail. But, at the same time, there are those outside as well as within their number who are concerned about those very buildings. In every Anglican diocese there is an advisory committee for the care of churches, and such committees often rightly have a strong conservation lobby in their membership. If a church receives a grant from English Heritage, that body will be concerned about any rearrangement of the interior that radically alters the character of the building. In our own century we have seen too much destruction of beautiful buildings to allow ourselves to be unconcerned about those that remain. Ireland and Scotland present us with many examples of old churches which have become sad ruins, while sometimes meaner Victorian substitutes are still in use. Since churches often represent the liturgical fashions of the days in which they were erected, and since such fashions have changed with the centuries, people are tempted to ask how permanent are the insights which we now claim as vital for worship, and whether what we now want to discard will be that for which our grandchildren will clamour.

We must nevertheless ask what needs can be identified as those of most modern congregations. First and foremost, there must be adequate provision for the ministry of the Word and Sacrament. As far as the altar or communion table is concerned, this needs to be central or free-standing, enabling the president with assistants or elders to take their places behind and around it; this is now the normal practice of most Christian denominations. Similarly, thought must be given to the siting and surrounding of the place of baptism. In Anglican churches, the traditional place for the font is near the door; but often it is hemmed in by pews and visible only to a section of the congregation, so that some churches adopt the expedient of a bowl on a small table when baptism is administered in the course of a Sunday service. But surely a church needs a visible representation of baptism at all times – which is perhaps another way of saying that in churches which practise infant baptism, there should be a proper font that is at least sometimes used. Lofty pulpits have gone out of fashion, as well as the oratorical style of preaching that went with them; often the pulpit is now no more than a lectern, and sometimes the same piece of furniture suffices for both the reading and preaching of the Word. But it still needs to be urged that whatever is used must be worthy of its purpose, and it is still desirable for the preacher to see (and be seen by) the congregation.

Two other needs may be more briefly stated. The building must be warm, cheerful, and provided with such seating as will prevent people thinking of how uncomfortable they are throughout the sermon. Unless it has adjacent buildings for the purpose, there is a need for toilet and coffee-making facilities. Finally, there is need for space and flexibility – to allow for ritual, drama, or dance. In any case, most churches are enhanced by space. A famous Anglican cleric of the first half of the twentieth century said "If you want to improve a church, take things out".

But very few congregations have the luxury of designing their own buildings or even paying for a substantial reordering of them. Most must make the most of what they have. Yet there are still things that can be done to avoid small congregations being scattered over acres of woodwork. One way is to use some part of the church that is suitable for the number of those present. In many Anglican churches, the chancel is quite big enough for early celebrations of Holy Communion or said evensongs. In some large churches, an aisle is curtained off and heated in the depths of winter. If funds permit, it is also possible and certainly desirable to adapt a part of the church for more flexible use, and so to make possible variety in the styles of worship. Large parish churches often have chapels that can be used in this way, and where a nave altar is the focal point of the church, the chancel may lend itself to such adaptation. Mention was made in an earlier chapter of the reordering of one small chapel in Gloucester Cathedral, so that there can be some variety in the way that the Eucharist is celebrated there. A URC church in the same county has an adjacent "little chapel" that is used for evening worship, and after the rebuilding of the City Temple in London, it was found necessary to have an alternative to "the great white pulpit".

As far as possible, it is important that the furnishings of these chapels or meeting places should be of the best quality that can be afforded. People quickly reject the experimental if it is always accompanied by the makeshift. And we should not be too ready to tolerate in church what we would not tolerate in our homes.

Some readers of this chapter may be wondering whether all this really matters, and what it has to do with growth. Surely the living God does not dwell in houses made with hands, and worship does not depend upon expensive equipment? Some will be quick to point out that the New Testament tells us nothing about buildings, and that congregations flourished and expanded without them. All this is true, but it has to be recognized that whereas the temple moved from a building to people in New Testament times, the focus returned to buildings not many centuries later.

We shall be returning in the next chapter to the balance that must be sought between stability and change. Here it is sufficient to emphasize again that we live in an age when the *visual* is of the greatest importance to the majority of people. The television and the video dominate many homes. What we see in church is therefore as important as what we hear; in some ways we have travelled back to the Middle Ages where the eye-gate was often the only gate. That is why the visual arrangements for worship are now so important. We must do our best to see that the signals sent out by our buildings and their arrangements are the signals that point to God as we believe him to have revealed himself. What people see when they worship can facilitate or stunt their growth.

PEOPLE

So we turn from the buildings to the people who worship in them. They may or may not grow through sheer attendance at worship, but they will grow as they understand more about it and as they participate in it.

By understanding worship, I do not mean that the whole congregation should become liturgical scholars. But many people do appreciate opportunities of learning more about the structure and history of the forms of worship in the churches to which they belong, as well as the practical arrangements (e.g. choice of hymns) that have to be made for the ordering of worship. And when changes are made, they are more receptive of them when they can see the reason for them.

But how can they get this sort of information? A series of
sermons is hardly the best method – for reasons which have been
urged in an earlier chapter. Suffice it now to summarize two of
them; first, the sermon is meant to be a breaking of the Word of
God, and, secondly, the whole subject of liturgy – practical as well
as theoretical – demands opportunities for question and discussion.
The smaller group, and certainly the less formal occasion, will
therefore be a more suitable setting. This means that only a fraction
of Sunday worshippers will take such an opportunity, but
sometimes this sort of information is better spread throughout the
congregation by small groups.

In the diocese of Gloucester, there has for some years been an
ecumenical project known as "Framework for Faith". It provides
basic courses for lay people on the Bible, Christian doctrine, and
worship in a number of centres, and it has proved to be an
enlarging experience for people from a variety of traditions. It was
followed by a shorter course called "Framework for Service" and
the liturgical part was meant to help those called to lead or
contribute to acts of worship – some of them for small groups of
people. Doubtless there are many other areas where similar
facilities exist.

Many congregations have a "worship committee" to keep their
worship constantly under review, and perhaps plan services for
certain special occasions. The value of such groups is two-fold;
first it can represent to those whose regular responsibility is the
ordering of worship the hopes, ideas, and wishes of those who
might not otherwise be heard. Secondly, the members can pass on
to others insights and information about the nature of worship, and
the constraints and opportunities which exist in their communities.
There are, however, certain dangers. The first is that the committee
can become too political, too concerned with winning victories for
certain pressure groups; the second is that it can become too local,
and unwilling to look for ideas beyond parochial or congregational
boundaries; and a third, arising from these two, is that members
suppose the only criterion in worship is what people *like*. It is
therefore important that members are willing to learn as well as to
express opinions; that it is broadly based so that the widest range of
needs is represented; and that there is a regular turnover in
membership of the committee.

Congregations are ceasing to be audiences or a set of
onlookers. It is now quite rare in Anglican churches for the
whole service to be "taken" by one person. Free Church services

are also less likely to be monologues, and since the Second Vatican Council, the Roman Catholic Church has involved its laity in reading lessons, leading intercessions, and administering Communion. I am aware of an Anglican parish which was without a vicar for well over a year, but the previous incumbent had set up a lay pastorate that was able to organize worship as well as to arrange visits to the sick and house-bound. Visiting clergy who came as preachers or presidents at the Eucharist were provided with concise and detailed instructions – which they might alter, but for which most were grateful. In another parish, however, the arrangements for Communion were in the hands of one person, and when she was suddenly taken ill, no one else knew where anything was kept.

Turning to oral leadership in worship, something has already been said about the importance of good reading of the Bible. For much of the twentieth century, reading the lessons was the only part of the service entrusted to the Anglican laity, and it was assumed that most people were capable of doing it. In fact, reading aloud in public is as skilled a matter as singing aloud in public; the group of people who read lessons are akin to the choir, and there is the same need for careful preparation and rehearsal. Lest it be thought that what has been written suggests an exclusive attitude to reading, it must be said that many people who would not have supposed themselves capable of reading aloud can be helped to do so, and the skilled are still capable of improvement. Just as there are additions to and retirements from the choir, so there should be to the group of people who read lessons.

In more recent years lay people have led intercessions, and perhaps other forms of prayer in the Roman and Anglican churches; and in the Free Churches, this may no longer be the invariable prerogative of the preacher. In response to this relatively new development, there have been a number of helpful handbooks for those who accept this responsibility and privilege.[1] There is room here for creativity and variety; the prayers can, for example, be led by more than one person, and from more than one part of the church. The all-important questions of audibility must determine all these arrangements, and those to whom this is entrusted must take care to keep within the time envisaged for this part of the worship.

When we speak of lay involvement in worship, we often think of how people can fulfil what has been conventional in our liturgies. We ought also to ask whether there are talents among members of the congregation that could enrich worship by contributing what has not been conventional in it. One illustration of this comes from the area of music. There is great variety in the instruments younger people have learned to play, and the report *In Tune with Heaven*[2] has a chapter concerned with musical instruments and equipment. An occasional anthem may be offered where there is a choir; but is there not also a place for a piano or oboe sonata? As the report itself says:

> *The provision of musical instruments in church should not be seen as solely for the accompaniment and embellishment of singing, but also for solo and ensemble playing before, during or after a service.*

Again, some congregations have sought to resolve the conflict that sometimes arises over the use of "modern" as opposed to "traditional" music by having two sets of people to offer different kinds of music – the organist and choir on the one hand, and the music group on the other.

But contribution to worship is not confined to the artistically gifted, and must be seen not to be so confined. Most churches have reason to be grateful to those whose contribution is more practical and manual – to voluntary cleaners, or those who have put their electrical knowledge or sonic skills at the disposal of the congregation. Churches have not always been good at identifying the wide variety of gifts and skills that may exist among their number, or giving them the high profile they deserve. I cannot forget the joy it gave to an elderly widower (by no means a regular worshipper) when asked to make a cross which would be suspended from the chancel arch during Holy Week.

People can grow as they exercise and develop their God-given talents, and as they realize that what they have to give is valued. But, as in everything else, growth can be stunted by human sin and pride. Some people can be content to do the same things in the same way and to suppose themselves incapable of improvement. And there are areas of church life which become little closed circles that are very difficult to enter. For example, flower arranging has become such a sophisticated art that the outsider can be frightened to offer her (or his) services. This will not happen if the person in charge is always on the look-out for recruits, and is willing to help and encourage the less skilled. We have been told repeatedly in recent years that we must not see children as the church of tomorrow, but as the church of today. The same is true of newcomers to a church, or newcomers to some form of service within it. Their function is not just to succeed those already engaged in the enterprise, but to participate in it themselves.

There are some churches where a few people do all the jobs; perhaps they are the only ones willing to undertake those jobs, and sometimes they complain that everything is left to "the same few". But sometimes this occurs because there has been no real attempt to draw others in, to encourage them to offer the gifts they have, or to exercise those gifts in their own way. The reason why some find it hard to delegate is that the delegated are seldom carbon copies of the delegators.

A quite different policy may be followed. As we noted earlier, it is not now easy to be an anonymous worshipper. Newcomers can be pounced upon and cajoled into some church activity for which they are not ready or for which they have no inclination. And those who resist such cajolements can feel guilty, or even be made to feel guilty. There are plenty of bad reasons why people draw back from what we will broadly call "activities" with the church. Among them are basic indifference to its mission, an unwillingness to be committed to anything, or a worldliness that does not give high priority to spiritual things. But there are also good reasons why some hesitate to come forward. This may have to do with the stage of pilgrimage through which people are passing. Perhaps they are very much "seekers", perhaps trying to grapple with the deep mysteries of faith, perhaps just needing a respite from church activities. Others cannot find anything on offer that seems to correspond with what they have to give – maybe because no one has helped them to identify their own contribution, or maybe because their local communities do not seem to want that contribution. Others still find their service to God lies quite outside the church structures – in local politics, or the Samaritans, or "meals on wheels". A woman pushing a pram told an archbishop that she didn't have much time for church work, but he pointed to the pram and said "There is your church work".

It is important that all Christians realize that they have "a calling to fulfil"; for some it lies dormant, and wise pastoral help will enable them to realize what it might be. It is no less important to remember that God calls in a limitless variety of ways, some which do not conform to our blinkered conception of him, or our equally blinkered idea of what his Church should be.

According to St Luke's Gospel, the good news of Christ's birth was first revealed to shepherds – the most unlikely people at that time.

Questions

1. How imaginatively are your buildings being used?

2. Discuss your policy for involving people in reading lessons.

3. In what way can the gifts of worshippers be discerned and encouraged?

Notes

1. For example, Paul Iles, *The Pleasure of God's Company* (Kevin Mayhew, 1990).

2. *In Tune with Heaven* (Church House Publishing with Hodder & Stoughton), section 410.

7 THE WOOD AND THE TREES

CHANGING WORLD AND UNCHANGING GOD

It is a commonplace to say that the rate of change in which we live is very hard for us to bear, that the inventions of the mind are so fast moving that our bodies and spirits can hardly keep up with them. It has sometimes been claimed that the people who lived in 1800 were nearer to New Testament times than we are to 1800. It is therefore not surprising that people turn to things of the past in their quest for continuity and stability – so cathedrals are visited and antique shops spring up in quite unlikely places. And it is equally not surprising that some look to religion, including the Christian religion, in the search for the same stability.

The Bible certainly speaks of God in these terms. He is the rock, the fortress, the one who does not change, the one to whom the people of the Old Testament are constantly exhorted to *return*. But it is important to remember that these are not the only ways in which God is described in the Old Testament. He is the one who goes before his people – cloud by day and fire by night. He is described in human terms as rising early to send the prophets, or as father, or husband. In recent years, theologians have pointed out feminine as well as masculine attributes in God. Often he is portrayed – perhaps to our embarrassment – as one who changes his mind, who is angry with his people, and then repents of his anger. Seldom is he conceived of as impassive, and never as aloof. In the New Testament, he is supremely, the one who sends his son, and is revealed in Jesus. The New Testament ends in the age of the Spirit – promised by Jesus as the one who would lead his people into new truth, and enable them to adapt to new situations, and to accept new challenges.

The variety of ways in which God is portrayed reminds us, in the first place, that we see God through the eyes of fallible men and women who were of like passions with us, however much they were inspired in their understanding of him. And this same variety reminds us that there is no single way of describing God – no formula that can sum up all his attributes. The Book of Job warns us of the impossibility of neat definitions. Christians believe that the most powerful and enduring way of describing God is by the word *Love* – but they find their faith in the twentieth century tested. No day passes without someone saying "If there is a God of love ... why?" We are concerned in this chapter not so much with the theology of God as with the worship of God. Many people look to worship as that which ought to embody all the truth about an unchanging God.When they worship, they hope to find that which is stable in our rapidly changing society. This is why changes in worship often meet with resentment and opposition.

CHANGING LITURGY

In the Anglican debates about the ordination of women to the priesthood, some people who ought to have known better were loud in their defence of what the Church has always taught and believed. In fact, it needs only a slight acquaintance with the history of the Church to realize that the word *always* can rarely be used about that history. This most certainly applies to the history of its worship. As an example of this, we may take the Book of Common Prayer – still by statute the official service book of the Church of England. Many people suppose it to have remained unchanged since the Act of Uniformity in 1662. The contents of the book may have remained more or less the same, but its uses have changed. From the first, it was supplemented by metrical psalms which never had the same authority, but which for over a century were probably the part of the service in which the congregation most obviously participated. In the eighteenth century, the rarity of Holy Communion was not envisaged by the book, and there is not much evidence of the invariable daily recitation of morning and evening prayer which it required. As the Catholic movement grew and developed in the second half of the following century, a whole number of additions to and subtractions from the services were found in many places – all unauthorized, and some the occasion of law-suits. The shortening of services was permitted in 1871, and doubtless practised in some places. Although the revision of the book in the 1920s proved abortive, many of the changes proposed in that revision found their way into the services of most parishes. So change there has certainly been – even though much of it came in by the back door. And when people now say that they want "the prayer book service" they do not mean that which is precisely set out in the 1662 book, but rather that version or adaptation of it with which they once found themselves familiar.

All this has happened in a church which seemed to have a fixed liturgy, and sometimes boasted of having it. So what of the churches not so committed? The history of worship in the church of Scotland, or in the Methodist or Reformed Churches in the UK shows much evolution, change, and adaptation. The early Baptists rejected the introduction of hymnody which, later, partly under Methodist influence, was to become the glory of the Free Churches. Chants and anthems, "lecturing" and children's addresses all had their day, and sometimes ceased to be. So now when people say that they like "a real Methodist service" they do not mean that which John Wesley conceived and ordered, but some form which they knew in their impressionable years – a form which had already changed and was in process of change.

None the less, the changes of the last half century have been more rapid and more drastic than any since the Reformation. Initially, some of the change was inspired by looking to the past rather than to the future. Anglicans asked what were the real intentions of the Book of Common Prayer, the Methodist Sacramental Fellowship looked to the high sacramental doctrines and practices of Wesley, Iona to the ideals of the Scottish reformers. But the ecumenical and liturgical movements walked hand in hand, and this resulted in a common search for origins and an agreement to look beyond the controversies of the Reformation era. In consequence, the pattern for the Eucharist in most churches has been that sketched by Justin Martyr in the second century, and the form of its central prayer has been based upon that of Hippolytus less than a century later.[1]

Students of liturgy tend to be interested most of all in its shape, but for many worshippers, the most dramatic and controversial change was in language. The use of modern language translations of the Bible led to a demand for modern language services; so words like "thou" and "dost" which had been used by English-speaking congregations since the Reformation, gave way to "you" and "does". What was new for Anglicans in the 1970s has become general in most churches in the 1990s.

In recent years, further questions have been asked about language. Since the publication of the Alternative Service Book in 1980, there has been a growing demand for "inclusive" language, and the rejection in some quarters of the word "man" as descriptive of the whole human race. New hymn books and collections of prayer have been sensitive to this issue. But deeper theological questions are raised when objections are made to the exclusive use of male images in connections with God himself, and the claim that at least some prayers should be addressed to "our mother God".

Liturgy has been slower in reflecting the widespread changes in our understanding of the world that have been brought about by scientific discovery. Albert Bayly was a pioneer among hymn writers searching for words that would enable people of our time to praise the Creator with integrity, and it has been mainly through hymnody and more occasional forms of prayer that so many contemporary concerns – ecology, world hunger, and peace – have been expressed. But more experimental liturgies have taken into account the mystery, complexity, and challenges of the world as we now perceive it.

The most interesting development for Anglicans, who in theory have had a fixed liturgy for 300 years, has been the very recent emphasis on flexibility and spontaneity. The report *Patterns for Worship* moved some way towards what is sometimes called the "directory" style of worship, in which rubrics prescribe what should be done, but allow wide selectivity in the contents of what is done. This report, together with the *The Promise of His Glory,* means that there can be considerable variety, both according to the seasons of the year and to local needs. Free Church people could be pardoned for supposing this to be a victory for some of those things for which they have contended, but they have, in all honesty, to remember that although their services have been in theory free compositions, in practice they have often followed a set pattern. "I often choose that for the second hymn" said a Methodist minister of a certain item, thereby implying that the character of the second hymn was always predetermined.

Few things are now quite predictable in worship, and we have passed the point where we thought we might draw up service books for a generation or even for a century. The ASB had 1980 deliberately stamped on its cover in order to emphasize that this was not the permanent alternative to the prayer book, and work has already begun on areas which need revision, and on the methods by which such revision might be undertaken. *The Methodist Service Book* of 1975 is soon to have a successor, and there have been two service books since the formation of the URC in 1972. A new *Book of Common Order* for the Church of Scotland in 1979 was replaced by another – and fuller – one in 1994.

Throughout the process we have been describing, it is unfortunate that the reformer and the traditionalist have often been at loggerheads. This has certainly happened in the matter of language. It has often been assumed that worship must either be entirely in antique or entirely in contemporary English. Thus, *Hymns for Today's Church*[2] claimed to be the obvious companion to the ASB because nearly all the hymns were "modernized" to fit in with the language and doctrines of that book. The Cathedral Close at Gloucester, like the cathedral itself, has a variety of styles of architecture, but that does not seem to destroy the harmony of either. Perhaps this could be applied to varieties of language within one act of worship. Nobody would applaud a prayer which began "O God, for as much as without thee, we are not able to please thee" and continued "Grant that your Holy Spirit may in all things direct and rule our hearts", but there is no reason why one prayer should not be in the "thou" form, and another in the "you" form. And certainly there has begun in the Church of England the search for a language that is richer and more resonant than that of much of the ASB.

OLD AND NEW

We are foolish if we ignore the way in which our forebears worshipped. We have noted that one phase of liturgical revision looked to the styles of worship they found in early centuries. We ought to look not only at the styles, but at the contents of worship in these and the centuries that followed. For this, three reasons may be advanced: first, the intrinsic beauty of some older liturgical material; secondly, because they may enshrine doctrines and insights that we have ignored; and thirdly, because the liturgies of the past link us with the worshippers of the past, and so enable us more vividly to apprehend the communion of saints.

The year 1992 witnessed the centenary of the birth of Bernard Lord Manning. Perhaps the most remarkable achievement of that remarkable man is to be found in the collection of five papers called *The Hymns of Wesley and Watts*, reprinted by Epworth Press as recently as 1988. Manning sought to recover, in the inter-war years, the treasures of doctrine and devotion that could be found in these hymns – and which were in danger of being overlooked in an age when *Songs of Praise* and *Worship Songs* were fashionable. As we saw in the last chapter, one generation often clamours for that which its predecessor sought to

discard. What Manning did in his day, others will do again – not
only for classical hymns, but also for the material to be found in
the prayer book and in the Authorized Version of the Bible. It is
interesting that in church music, some Victorian compositions that
were scorned in the first half of the twentieth century have been
recalled in the second.

But alongside what is old, there must be that which is new –
completely new. Users of the ASB have often commented that the
new prayers written for that book are more effective than the old
ones which have been "modernized". The same is generally true of
hymnody – though a little invisible mending can render singable
what might have been discarded because of one grotesque line or
phrase. We must have the courage to believe that the Holy Spirit is
still guiding and directing us, and that there was no cut-off point in
history at which inspiration finally ceased. It was said of the great
hymnologist, Erik Routley, that he loved the hymns of the past so
much that he encouraged those of the present, believing that
the inspiration of Watts and Doddridge must continue beyond
Wren and Dudley-Smith. Each generation must make its own
contribution to liturgy; part of that contribution will be for its own
day and will be quickly dated, other parts will find their way into
continuing acts of praise and prayer, and a further part will be
eclipsed for a while and then rediscovered.

The thesis that I am seeking to advance is that old and new can
exist side by side, as indeed they do in so many of our hymn books.
Collections like *Hymns and Psalms*, *Rejoice and Sing*, or the new
standard version of *Hymns Ancient and Modern* provide lessons
for the rest of liturgy. Maybe in some future ASB, the Prayer
Book collects could be left in that form alongside those more
recently composed, and passages from the Authorized Version
join those from newer translations. In the Book of Revelation,
God is more than once worshipped in three tenses – the one who
was, who is, and who is to come. Those same tenses must be
represented in our liturgy – that which links us to our fellow
worshippers in past ages, that which asserts the sovereignty of
God over the here and now, and that which is straining forward to
what he will do, and to the kingdom which is yet to be fulfilled.

Without all three tenses, there is something lop-sided about our
worship, and perhaps lop-sided about our faith. Those who refuse
to have anything but traditional worship may have fallen into the
danger of trying to lock God up in the past. Those who ignore the
past are rejecting not only a dimension of Christian experience, but

falling into the error of supposing themselves wiser than any generation that has lived. The danger of a religion or worship that is focused on the future has become so apparent to us in the twentieth century that we have been frightened of any reference to it at all, lest it deflect us from our present duties on earth. But the favourite tense of the Bible seems to be that future, and the early Eucharists were seen not only as a memorial of what had happened, but also as an anticipation of what would happen – what the present Methodist service book calls "the heavenly banquet prepared for all mankind".

SORTING IT OUT

The title of this chapter was chosen because there are many who find themselves confused about what seem rapid changes in liturgy when they themselves are looking for some stability in a rapidly changing world. The title is also worth keeping in mind when liturgy is discussed at a local level. There are churches where small amendments to worship are more contentious than those which are considerable. Arguments of some heat can arise over matters of secondary or even trivial importance, rather than over major considerations. Reading this book will not resolve such arguments, but it may be useful at this stage to ask what seem to be essential elements in Christian worship.

Two chapters have dealt at some length with the reading and preaching of the Word of God, and with the celebration of the sacraments of baptism and Holy Communion. But within worship there will be various forms of prayer, and to these we now turn.

There are endless ways in which public and private prayer can be classified, but I offer five which are common to most liturgies, and probably to more informal styles of worship.

1. *Praise and adoration.* This is likely to be most significantly expressed in singing, and that will be the specific concern of the last chapter. But praise and adoration may be spoken as well as sung, and may take the form of prayers, litanies, or canticles for choral speaking.

2. *Penitence.* Any liturgy that has focused on the holiness of God will, in response, include the penitence of the congregation who have fallen short of his glory. Sometimes, this will be in the form of prayer offered by the leader of worship, but more often there

will be an opportunity for the worshippers to express penitence in a prayer or litany of confession. This is followed by an "absolution" or declaration of God's forgiveness.

3. *Intercession.* This was once most often represented by a series of collects in Anglican worship, and by the "long prayer", of the Free Churches. It now more often includes responsive material such as "Lord, in your mercy/hear our prayer". There are other possibilities of biddings and responses which can be found in the books already mentioned. Intercession will include the needs of the church, the world, the local community, the suffering, and (in some traditions) the departed.

4. *Thanksgiving.* Sometimes in Anglican worship, this element has been least conspicuous, or offered in too general a form. It should surely balance those concerns for which intercession is offered (e.g. prayers for the sick can be balanced with thanksgiving for health and healers), and for this reason it is sometimes good to combine those two kinds of prayer.

5. *Dedication.* Most forms of worship will need to include some renewal of our dedication to God. This is usually the burden of the prayer offered after communion but it is needed at other times. It may be expressed in a hymn; and in some traditions the dedication of the offerings includes the dedication of those who make them.

As suggested above, there is a variety of ways in which these forms of prayer may be offered. But for those who draw up services and those who are monitoring the regular worship of their churches, it is useful to have some sort of check-list that will enable them to ensure worship is balanced. In churches of several traditions, an agreed structure with varied content now seems to be the practice. Some worshippers need forms of prayer which are regularly recited, and into which they can slot their own penitence, thanksgiving, or intercession. Others find that set forms of words quickly become stale, and have been said before the worshipper has begun to think of them. This may be a matter of temperament, but probably most of us need both. What has been written about old and new may have implications for this aspect of worship. There is a place for the tried and the familiar, and there is a place for the fresh and unfamiliar. Both can contribute to our growth. If we reject one, we ought to ask why, and to consider whether we are missing something that God wants to show us. Perhaps the one could be missing new insights and challenges, and the other be evading that perseverance that must remain part of our Christian calling.

Sometimes we need to be confronted, sometimes to be challenged. Sometimes we need to receive new things, sometimes to persevere in old things. In the worship of God, we find these needs addressed. And all can be part of our growth:

> *To thee we rise, in thee we rest;*
> *We stay at home, we go in quest,*
> *Still thou art our abode.*
> *The rapture swells, the wonder grows,*
> *As full on us new life still flows*
> *From our unchanging God.*

Questions

1. How balanced is the worship of your church?

2. What are the best ways to introduce change?

3. How practicable is all-age worship?

Notes

1. Kenneth Stevenson, *The First Rites* (Marshall Pickering, 1989), offers a simple and helpful comparison of early and present-day Christian worship.

2. *Hymns for Today's Church* (Hodder & Stoughton, 1982).

8 THE PRAISE OF GOD'S PEOPLE

PRAISE SITS SILENT

Much has been written in this book about the words which are spoken in worship, and before we turn to what is sung, it would be appropriate to say something about silence. Isaac Watts and the Wesleys were prolific hymn writers, but a hymn of Watts, much altered by John Wesley, bases its last verse on Ecclesiastes 5.2:

> God is in heaven, we dwell below;
> Be short our tunes, our words be few;
> A sacred reverence checks our songs,
> And praise sits silent on our tongues.

Most congregations are frightened of silence. Anglican organists wonder whether the hymn will be long enough to "cover" the offertory. In some Free Churches where it is customary to take up the collection during organ music, there is further improvisation after its dedication. But individual members of congregations are often equally afraid of silence. It is prized and cherished by a few, but when leaders of worship plan silence, they need to remember that many people never experience it. There is always music or talking in the background. It is essential therefore that people are *helped* to use silence.

It is certainly important before worship. A buzz or roar of conversation now seems an inevitable prelude to every church service. We are not likely to go back to the days when people simply did not talk in church, and not many would want us to do so. But somewhere there needs to be a cut-off point, and a period of silence observed; perhaps it should be after the ministers and choir have entered as they can be the worst offenders; perhaps, in view of what has been written above, there should be something on which all can focus – a lighted candle, or the bringing in and opening of the Bible.

Many of our newer services suggest periods of silence in the course of worship, and the collection *Lent, Holy Week, Easter*[1] prescribes it for some services. It provides an opportunity after readings or sermons to reflect upon what has been said, or after the eucharistic prayer to reflect upon what has been done. In the course of prayers, it allows people to add their own. And, always, it gives a certain breathing space to acts of worship, helping us to appreciate depths in ourselves, in what we are doing, and to remember that no words or music or ritual are adequate for the God whom we seek to worship.

HYMNS

We turn now to that medium of praise which is most common to us all. In almost every church you go to, you will be handed a hymn book. Roman Catholics are among the latest to use hymns in their normal Sunday service. They came into Anglicanism in a variety of ways and, before the days of the ASB, no one was quite sure of their legality. But they have often been the part of the service in which the congregation feels most confident in its participation – as it did in the metrical psalms which preceded conventional hymnody. By and large, in all churches which stem from the Reformation, hymns have played an important part in liturgy. Methodism, in a famous phrase "was born in song", and the various styles of revival have usually been accompanied by new bursts of hymnody.

I wrote at length in *The Use of Hymns* about the purposes which they fulfil, and will do no more than summarize those purposes now. Hymns are an obvious means of congregational participation; they underline doctrine and reflect in song that which can never fully be explained; they express experience, and set forth what is involved in the Christian pilgrimage; in some parts of the Church, they adorn liturgy, while in others they have been an integral part of the liturgy itself.

For such high purposes, we need the best texts that can be devised, and the best tunes that can be composed. This does not mean that hymns should qualify as poetry; there are some hymns that find their way into anthologies of verse, and there are some poems which lend themselves to singing. But there is a difference of function between the two; poems are normally meant to be read, silently or aloud, by one person; hymns are normally meant to be

sung by a collection of people. What has been designed for
this second purpose usually lasts rather longer than that which
has been adapted to it; *Songs of Praise* and, more recently, the
The Cambridge Hymnal provide many examples of fine poetry that
have never quite "taken off" as hymns.

But hymns still need to be of the best. They need to be
theologically and grammatically acceptable. If they are to mean anything to those who sing them, they need to have at least one line that
is memorable. "Abide with me" may owe some of its popularity to
Monk's "Eventide" and some to its use at great sporting events; but
some of that popularity surely derives from the memorable phrases
with which it is packed. But to return to the main point about
acceptability; people will argue *ad infinitum* about the theological
credentials of a hymn, and our attitudes usually depend upon our
own theological stance. Judgements on syntax or scansion will
depend upon the age group to which we belong or the kind of
education we have received. Very few hymns will be thought good
by everyone; but that should not prevent anyone from asking these
questions about the hymns we sing. Asking such questions will mean
some study of the hymn that goes beyond its first line. Some hymns
are too quickly dismissed because they are not immediately
understood. Someone recently complained that "New every morning
is the love" was world denying (God will provide for sacrifice),
whereas it is just the opposite.

The holy God whom we worship calls for the best that we can
offer but he is the one who became incarnate, and shared our life in
this world. This surely means that hymns, or some of them, can be
homely and personal, and that we can properly sing of the concerns
of this world that God loves. *The Methodist Hymn Book* of 1933
said, moreover, that some hymns had been selected chiefly because
they were "dear to the people of God".

This leads us, inevitably, to what might be called "alternative
hymnody", to what is contained in those many volumes of songs
and choruses that are found on the shelves of religious bookshops.
Many churches now want what is often misnamed "a modern
hymn book" alongside their more traditional standard collections,
and indeed such "modern" items are finding their way into the
standard collections themselves. But the whole matter can be and
has been a cause of dissension in many congregations, leading to
the resignation of organists and others as well. To those who are
enthusiastic about this sort of material, I would merely suggest that
they do not ignore the centuries of devotion that we find in

classical hymnody – for reasons outlined in the last chapter. That chapter also had a word for those who are less than enthusiastic about this genre of Christian song. Some who have been associated mainly with traditional music – such as the Royal School of Church Music and the proprietors of *Hymns Ancient and Modern*[2] are now encouraging us to look for the best in these freer styles of hymn, and we might find that good material here could supplant bad material in our traditional collections. Hymns have played a modest but significant part in the ecumenical development of the twentieth century; it would be tragic if differences in hymn styles led to new forms of division.

Hymns do much for us. They can comfort and restore us, they can strengthen and enlarge us. But they also make demands upon us. They require the use of our voices. Many people say they cannot sing, but some could if they were given help. All who do sing need to give the text and the tune their full attention, to be on their feet with books open before it begins, to draw breaths at suitable moments (an occasional hymn practice or "Songs of Praise" may help here), so to sing as to make sense of the words and to make sense of the mood or moods of the hymn. The hymn also requires the use of our minds; great hymns will often enlarge our understanding and inspire our imagination, and some ought to stretch us. A recent writer, recognizing that many people learn their theology through hymns, has suggested that they might be the subject matter of discussion groups, and has given some useful illustrations of how this could work.[3] This means that we often have to work at both words and music, and worshippers should be encouraged to have their own hymn books at home. Texts on a screen will be useful for certain occasions, but people are less likely to make them part of themselves. Thirdly, and most important of all, hymns require the offering of the heart, since they raise and quicken the spirit of devotion. But this third requirement of hymnody is not likely to be met if the first two are ignored.

It will be obvious from what has been written here that hymns involve both the adoration of God and the edification of his people. A balance between the two needs to be maintained in the choice of hymns. There are some hymns in which members of the congregation seem to be addressing one another, as in "Brother, sister, let me serve you" – which has become popular in recent years. In "Will your anchor hold in the storms of life?" the congregation asks itself rhetorical questions, but supplies affirmations in the chorus. Other hymns express Christian reflection on the nature and works of God, and only some are directly addressed to him. A similar balance is needed between what people like and enjoy, and what helps them to explore further stages of pilgrimage; hence, it would always be disastrous to have all the hymns in a service chosen by popular vote.

I cannot conclude this section without reiterating the point which was my main reason for writing *The Use of Hymns*. This concerns careful choice. I believe that people will always sing, appreciate, and benefit from hymns that seem right for the occasion, that are appropriate for the point in the liturgy for which they are chosen, that relate to what is the basic theme of the service and the preacher, and which thus become an integral part of the worship. Part of the "goodness" of a "good" hymn is experienced only when it is sung at the right time and place.

INSTRUMENTS AND VOICES

Hymns are the main common factor of praise in the churches, but other forms of singing occur in the liturgy. Among Anglicans, there has long been the custom of singing at matins and evensong responses, and chants to canticles and psalms, and at the Eucharist such parts as the Gloria and Sanctus. Some of the music in parish churches has been modelled on that of cathedrals and, in our own twentieth century, this imitation has been questioned. Chants are less common in the Free Churches, but are by no means unknown; they are provided in the standard hymn books of most denominations. A rather curious practice in some Free Churches has been singing of the Lord's Prayer to a fairly elaborate setting by the whole congregation.

Newer liturgies provide for greater congregational participation, and the acclamations found in most eucharistic prayers have encouraged musicians to compose settings for them. From Iona and Taizé came the custom of using music in prayers – either as a response to it, or as background to the spoken words. This sort of material is again finding its way into service books and hymnals. The possibilities of congregational participation in music may be greater now than at any time in history. A recent writer on the Anglican daily office has advocated the singing of many parts of it, even with a small number and without accompaniment.[4]

And there are still those items in which part of the congregation (e.g. the choir) sings to the remainder – anthems, or motets, or solos. It needs to be emphasized that this is also part of worship –

both by those who play and sing, and by those who listen. This can too easily be regarded as a sort of sacred entertainment, and the efforts of instrumentalists treated as a background for chat. It must also be emphasized that participation can be by ear as well as by voice. The singing of psalms by a trained choir can enable the rest of the congregation to attend to their meaning, often to gain new insights from them, and so to be enriched by the experience. The same applies to anthems – where music illustrates texts of scripture, prayers, or poems. Some of the considerations which have been advanced about hymns need to be applied here. The texts and music must be appropriate to Christian worship, and to the particular services at which they are sung. And most people in the congregation will derive greater benefit from the anthem if they know *what* is being sung.

PSALMS

We must give some attention to the most ancient source of praise for Christian people – the book of psalms. The New Testament suggests that they were, from the earliest days, used in Christian worship and devotion. They formed the staple part of the office in the medieval church, and the Reformation of the sixteenth century sought to recover them for the congregation. The Anglican Prayer Book ordered them to be read (or sung) through in their entirety each month – that is, twelve times as often as other parts of the Old Testament. Moreover, as we have noted, metrical versions were appended to the Prayer Book, and the psalms in metre became the principal form of the congregational praise in many of the Reformed Churches.

At the end of the twentieth century, the Psalter is far less well known than it was at the beginning. This is certainly true for Anglicans, and one reason for it is the decline of matins and evensong on Sundays. The most popular forms of worship in the Church of England are:

- some form of parish Eucharist – the services in the ASB provide for psalmody and appoint portions of it for Sundays, but it is not mandatory and is frequently omitted;

- the family service which is not likely to include any extended form of psalmody.

To all this we must add the diminution of choirs, the dearth of organists, and the manifold difficulties for congregations in singing anything but the simplest metrical versions.

In 1973, the Church of Scotland broke with tradition in including both metrical and prose versions of the psalms in the third edition of the *Church Hymnary*. The editors hoped that this would encourage a fuller use of the psalms, but for many this seemed a downgrading of the psalter which had traditionally been bound in separate covers and treated as something separate from hymns. Broadcast services from the kirk do not suggest the traditional practice of opening worship with a metrical psalm or even the invariable inclusion of one within the service.

When writing on this subject a few years ago, I suggested a number of different ways in which the psalms might be sung, but since that time more and more people have been alerted to the danger of losing them. The Royal School of Church Music has encouraged at local and national level festivals in which they are used in a variety of ways. In 1990, Jubilate Hymns produced *Psalms for Today and Songs from the Psalms,*[5] where they are set to chants, sung in metre, presented responsorially, or provided with chorus – this making them usable for churches with choirs, or music groups, or for churches with neither. A year later, Bible Society published a smaller selection, *Sing Psalms*[6] taken from the Good News and New International versions of the Bible with settings by a group of composers, and an introduction by Bishop Colin Buchanan, which is characteristically perceptive and persuasive.

The most encouraging essay in this direction, in my view, is provided by the 90 items which form the psalms and canticles section of the hymn book *Rejoice and Sing.*[7] Again, there is variety in the ways in which the psalms may be sung – chants, tones, responsorially, and in metre. But, unlike the books mentioned in the last paragraph, there is variety also in the translations that have been used. Thus items come from the Scottish Psalter of 1650, and from the pens of Isaac Watts, Ian Pitt-Watson, John Bell, and Tate and Brady – to mention only some of those who have contributed to the metrical part of it. This points the way to what might be undertaken by the churches as an ecumenical exercise – a common psalter for worship with a large selection of psalms of various styles and from various translations. Here could be that combination of old and new that was recommended in the last chapter.

Great stress has been laid on variety in the use of psalms, and for this there is good reason. Nothing must be allowed to obscure the rich and manifold variety that is within the psalter. Something of that variety can be missed if they are all translated by one small group, and something can be missed if they are always said or sung in the same way. The conventional Anglican method of reciting the psalms can make them all sound the same.

I hope it is not necessary to defend the use of the psalms or to say here why they are valuable for Christian devotion. The witness of many centuries can be joined to the witness of the last decade, and the efforts to recover their use which we have noted. The psalms are still not lacking in apologists and expositors, and people are still setting them afresh, and producing new versions of them. Almost everybody would agree that a certain selectivity is needed for Sunday use, and some would advocate the same policy for a weekday office. Sometimes paraphrases of them go beyond that which the psalmist intended, and Isaac Watts recommended a thorough Christianization of them, and sought to provide it. Perhaps this is, once again, not so much a question of either/or, but of both/and. We can join ancient Israel in its yearning for the Messiah's kingdom (Psalm 72) and yet rejoice in the affirmation:

> *Jesus shall reign, wher'er the sun*
> *Does his successive journeys run.*

GROWTH THROUGH PRAISE

After this survey of some of the material that might be used by congregations in their praise, we must go on to ask the question which is central to this book: how will it enable them to grow? This, in part, depends upon their understanding of what they sing, the extent to which they have made it their own, and the way in which it has become transparent of the things of God which it seeks to extol. For all this, I offer five suggestions.

1. It is helpful from time to time in worship to indicate why a particular hymn is being sung, or what is the basic thrust of a psalm to be used. This is a method that must be used sparingly if it is not to become tedious. Sometimes, people must be allowed to make their own discoveries.

2. A sermon can sometimes be preached about a hymn, and certainly about a psalm. A short course of sermons could be offered on a wide selection of hymns, or there could be a course on a psalm, hymn, canticle, or chorus. This often has considerable appeal for congregations, but, again, must not be repeated too often for it will not meet the needs of all worshippers.

3. The members of the congregation should, as I suggested earlier, be encouraged to have their own hymn books, and to use during the week the notice sheet that records the hymns and readings. This will enable them to work over the material in the ways that some Puritans did with the sermon – calling the exercise, "chewing the cud".

4. It might be possible to encourage the use of some simple "daily office" (avoiding the phrase where it might be offputting). However, a structure of psalm – reading – hymn – prayer could be helpful to individuals, at house groups, or at the end of meetings.

5. Brief reference has already been made to "Songs of Praise", and by the use of this title, I do not mean the precise format of the present BBC 1 programme where people are interviewed with a series of attractive scenes of the local beauty spot in the background. There may be occasions for both at a local level, but by this title I mean a service that is centred around praise. This kind of service does attract to church some who are not there regularly, so it could involve the growth of people – both within themselves as well as growth in their numbers. It gives people the chance to sing their "favourite" hymns, to hear more about them, and so to sing with understanding as well as the spirit. It is a way of introducing new items and provides a relaxed way of learning them; a musician with tact and skill will help people to discover that it is actually more fun to sing things well than to sing them badly. The role of the "presenter" is no less important, for this can be a learning excercise at a number of levels. This format could be used up to six times a year – especially if some occasions could be focused on a Christian festival, or a natural season recognized by all. For the sake of newcomers, and those who have not yet been persuaded to buy their own hymn books, and in order to include material from other sources, it is an advantage to have a special service sheet, and a further advantage to have the treble line of the

music for the hymns. Most hymn books have directions about what is under copyright, and how permission to reproduce it may be sought. People sometimes say that they heard and liked a hymn on a particular occasion, but cannot remember what it is. So, another advantage of this service sheet is that they can take it away with them, and this could be the beginning of them making the hymns their own.

PRAISING A MYSTERY

Much has been written about the need for mystery in worship, and the absence of it has often been deplored. The conclusion of this book is hardly the appropriate place to explore such a theme, but in that context, two things need to be said.

First, our worship must express the mystery of life itself. In cheerful songs we can all join, but neither our songs nor other parts of worship should evade the tragedies and unresolved questions of life; the psalms again serve as a model here – with their laments as well as their jubilation, their questionings as well as their serenity.

Secondly, worship must point to mysteries beyond us; worship does indeed open a door into heaven, but we can see only a little of what lies beyond it. The God whom we know is yet to be known. This chapter opened with a reference to a text from Ecclesiastes, and ends with some verses from the Apocrypha, and the book called Ecclesiasticus:

> *However much we may say, our words will fall short;*
> *the end of the matter is: God is all.*
> *Where can we find the skill to sing his praise?*
> *For he is greater than all his works.*
> *Honour the Lord to the best of your ability*
> *yet still is he high above all praise.*
> *Summon all your strength to extol him,*
> *and be untiring, for you will always fall short.*
> *Who has seen him, that he can describe him?*
> *Can anyone praise him as he truly is?*
> *We have seen but a small part of his works,*
> *and there remain many mysteries greater still.*

Questions

1. What are the main gaps in your hymn book?

2. Discuss the best way of using psalms in your church.

3. How is it possible to combine a warm and friendly
    atmosphere with one of stillness and reverence?

Notes

1. *Lent, Holy Week, Easter* (Church House Publishing, Cambridge
    University Press, SPCK, 1984, 1986).

2. For example, *Worship Songs Ancient & Modern* (Canterbury Press,
    1992).

3. Brian Castle, *Sing a New Song to the Lord* (DLT, 1994), see
    especially Chapter 4.

4. George Guiver, *Company of Voices* (SPCK, 1988).

5. *Psalms for Today* and *Songs from the Psalms* (Hodder & Stoughton,
    1990).

6. *Sing Psalms* (Bible Society, 1991).

7. *Rejoice & Sing* (Oxford University Press, 1991).

GEORGIANA